Digital Education and Learning

Series Editor
Michael Thomas, Liverpool John Moores University, Merseyside, UK

Much has been written during the first decade of the new millennium about the potential of digital technologies to produce a transformation of education. Digital technologies are portrayed as tools that will enhance learner collaboration and motivation and develop new multimodal literacy skills. Accompanying this has been the move from understanding literacy on the cognitive level to an appreciation of the sociocultural forces shaping learner development. Responding to these claims, the Digital Education and Learning Series explores the pedagogical potential and realities of digital technologies in a wide range of disciplinary contexts across the educational spectrum both in and outside of class. Focusing on local and global perspectives, the series responds to the shifting landscape of education, the way digital technologies are being used in different educational and cultural contexts, and examines the differences that lie behind the generalizations of the digital age. Incorporating cutting edge volumes with theoretical perspectives and case studies (single authored and edited collections), the series provides an accessible and valuable resource for academic researchers, teacher trainers, administrators and students interested in interdisciplinary studies of education and new and emerging technologies.

Maria Ranieri · Stefano Cuomo ·
Gabriele Biagini

Artificial Intelligence in School

A Pedagogical Framework for Critical AI Literacy

palgrave
macmillan

Maria Ranieri
University of Florence
Florence, Italy

Stefano Cuomo
University of Florence
Florence, Italy

Gabriele Biagini
University of Florence
Florence, Italy

ISSN 2753-0744 ISSN 2753-0752 (electronic)
Digital Education and Learning
ISBN 978-3-032-15918-2 ISBN 978-3-032-15919-9 (eBook)
https://doi.org/10.1007/978-3-032-15919-9

Translation from the Italian language edition: "Scuola e intelligenza artificiale. Percorsi di alfabetizzazione critica" by Maria Ranieri et al., © Carocci editore S.p.a. 2024. Published by Carocci editore S.p.a.. All Rights Reserved.

This Palgrave Macmillan imprint is published by the registered company Springer Nature Switzerland AG
The registered company address is: Gewerbestrasse 11, 6330 Cham, Switzerland

This book was jointly conceived, carried out, and revised by the authors. In terms of text editing, Chapters The Dimensions of Artificial Intelligence Literacy: A Pedagogical Perspective and Conclusion: Implementing AI Literacy in Schools—A Roadmap for Educators *were jointly authored by M. Ranieri, S. Cuomo, and G. Biagini. S. Cuomo authored* Chapter The Cognitive Dimension: Historical Background and Key Concepts, *G. Biagini* Chapter The Operational Dimension: Uses and Applications, *M. Ranieri* Chapter The Ethical Dimension: General Principles and Educational Perspectives. *For* Chapter The Critical Dimension: Understanding and Evaluation Beyond Automation *M. Ranieri is the author of* Sects. 1.1 and 2.1 and *G. Biagini* Sects. 1.2 and 2.2.

Preface

Until not long ago, the term "Artificial Intelligence" (AI) was largely restricted to experts and technology specialists, whereas today it has entered common usage. A simple query on Google Trends suffices to illustrate the growing interest in the topic over the past five years, with a gradual rise between 2020 and 2022 (interest index of approximately 33 and 40, respectively) followed by a substantial surge between 2023 and 2025 (around 71 and 100, respectively). Discussions on the topic appear every day in news outlets and television reports, sometimes envisioning a dystopian future of humans subjugated to machines, sometimes extolling a new revolution on the wave of yet another technological hype under the banner of the triumphalist faith in inevitable progress. The subject is a matter of scholarly debate not only for technicians, but also for philosophers, sociologists, or education scholars. Here, too, one often finds traces of a long-standing debate, animated by apodictic oppositions reminiscent of those that have long dominated reflection on the relationship between education and technologies (Ranieri, 2019a): starting from an essentialist view of technology, such positions adopt deterministic readings of its social impact on society—either optimistic (technology as the panacea of society's ills) or pessimistic (technology is the cause of all society's ills)—while neglecting the salience of extra-technological factors such as politics, economics, and social structures (Buckingham, 2007).

Despite growing interest, AI is not new. It is a field of research that—with ups and downs (the so-called "AI winters")—has been studied for some seventy years, and its applications have long animated the digital ecosystem with which we interact every day. Querying a search engine, automatically translating a text, interacting with a voice assistant, and even the small robot that cleans the floors of our homes rely—more or less—on applications of AI.

Explaining the reasons for this new *springtime* of AI requires considering not only the technology but also broadening the analysis to include social, political, and economic aspects, which are beyond the scope of this volume.[1] We can, however, say that while the hype surrounding AI will likely subside, it will not diminish the impact this technology will have on our societies and daily lives. As happened previously with the spread of the personal computer, then the Internet, and again mobile phones, AI is poised to become a new actor in the world of digital technologies. In the face of this unprecedented scenario, what can be the role of educators and teachers, especially those who work with younger learners? Can the education system postpone engagement with these issues until upper secondary or university education, or should they be addressed from the earliest stages of schooling?

Institutionally, an initial indication for answering this question comes from the European Recommendation on Key Competences for Lifelong Learning, which has included digital competences since 2006 (European Commission, 2006). These have been defined analytically through the *DigComp* framework (Ferrari et al., 2014), which, in its latest version, also includes AI. In other words, according to the European legislator, citizens of the new millennium must master the informed use of digital technologies—including AI—for education, work, leisure, socialisation, and civic participation. A further indication, which helps to compose the picture and formulate a response, comes from *DigCompEdu* (Redecker, 2017), the framework that defines the roles, functions, and competences of teachers and educators in digital matters: teachers' digital competences include those related to the promotion of students' digital skills. It follows that basic education—entrusted to schools and teachers must take responsibility for preparing students in the field of AI.

From a research perspective, the answer to the question concerning the role of schools in addressing these issues should be situated within

[1] In this regard, some readings are suggested such as Elliott (2021), Mitchell (2020), Russell (2020) or even Crawford (2021).

the scholarship on *new literacies* (Cappello, 2017; Ranieri, 2019b), to which the "digital turn" (Mills, 2010, p. 246) has given considerable impetus. The increased attention to new literacy practices that have developed in digital environments has expanded the traditional concept of literacy, encompassing not only printbased reading and writing, but also the comprehension and production of new textualities, as well as mediated forms of communication and interaction for meaning-making. Put differently, the emergence of new digital textualities—through wikis, blogs, databases, and online news—calls for new skills in text comprehension alongside abilities to craft and communicate digital productions. In this context, we emphasise the importance of education that takes into account the new forms of literacy required by digital society, including AI literacy—for example, consider Floridi's (2025) notion of "distant writing"—, and we endorse schooling as a site where students can acquire the skills needed to critically navigate an increasingly digitised world, while safeguarding human values and promoting a more equitable and inclusive future (Selwyn et al., 2023; Wilton et al., 2022).

Thus, by bringing together the institutional and research perspectives, we can conclude that the answer to the question of whether schools should deal with AI from the earliest stage of education turns out to be affirmative. The challenge then becomes to define on what terms it should be addressed—precisely what we attempt in this volume—adopting a pedagogical perspective, that is, one attentive to dimensions that are pedagogically salient for critical AI literacy. In line with our previous studies on digital competence (Calvani et al., 2012), the focus will be placed not on technical minutiae but on the pedagogical aspects involved in understanding the basic concepts of AI, the mechanisms that characterise its operation, the social and cognitive implications of human-computer interaction, and the contentious—often ethical—issues associated with its application. Indeed, the pedagogical dimension concerns the critical-cognitive infrastructure that the educational work on AI, taken as an object of learning for citizenship, can solicit and foster. From this point of view, the volume offers theoretical elements for reflecting on the themes invoked as well as educational activities that teachers and educators can implement with their students in order to learn to engage critically and consciously with AI technologies and to be prepared, as citizens, to discuss openly and democratically AI's role in our societies.

Florence, Italy
July 2025

Maria Ranieri

References

Buckingham, D. (2007). *Beyond technology: Children's learning in the age of digital culture*. Cambridge: Polity Press.

Calvani, A., Fini, A., Ranieri, M., & Picci, P. (2012). Are young generations in secondary school digitally competent? A study on Italian teenagers. *Computers & Education, 58*, 797–807. https://doi.org/10.1016/j.compedu.2011.10.004

Cappello, G. (2017). Literacy, media literacy and social change. Where do we go from now? *Italian Journal of Sociology of Education, 9*(1), 31–44.

Crawford, K. (2021). *Atlas of AI: Power, Politics, and the Planetary Costs of Artificial Intelligence*. Yale University Press.

Elliott, A. (Ed.). (2021). *The Routledge social science handbook of AI* (1st ed.). Routledge.

European Commission. (2006). *Recommendation of the European Parliament and of the Council of 18 December 2006 on key competences for lifelong learning (2006/962/EC).* Official Journal of the European Union, L 394/1–18.

Ferrari, A., Brecko, B., & Punie, Y. (2014). *DIGCOMP: A framework for developing and understanding digital competence in Europe*. Luxembourg: Publications Office of the European Union.

Floridi, L. (2025). Distant writing: Literary production in the age of artificial intelligence (Rev. version 5, April 26, 2025). *Centre for Digital Ethics (CEDE) Research Paper.* https://doi.org/10.2139/ssrn.5232088

Mills, K. A. (2010). A review of the "digital turn" in the new literacy studies. *Review of Educational Research, 80*(2), 246–271. https://doi.org/10.3102/0034654310364401

Mitchell, M. (2020). *Artificial Intelligence: A Guide for Thinking Humans*. Picador USA.

Ranieri, M. (2019a). Teaching with media. In R. Hobbs & P. Mihailidis (Eds.-in-Chief), G. Cappello, M. Ranieri, & B. Thevenin (Assoc. Eds.), The international encyclopedia of media literacy (pp. 1–11). Hoboken, NJ: John Wiley & Sons, Inc. https://doi.org/10.1002/9781118978238.ieml0233

Ranieri, M. (2019b). Literacy, technology, and media. In R. Hobbs & P. Mihailidis (Eds.-in-Chief), G. Cappello, M. Ranieri, & B. Thevenin (Assoc. Eds.), *The international encyclopedia of media literacy* (pp. 1–12). Hoboken,

NJ: John Wiley & Sons, Inc. https://doi.org/10.1002/9781118978238.iem10100

Redecker, C. (2017). *European framework for the digital competence of educators: DigCompEdu*. Luxembourg: Publications Office of the European Union. https://doi.org/10.2760/178382

Russell, S. (2020). *Human compatible: Artificial intelligence and the problem of control* (3rd ed.). London: Penguin Putnam Inc.

Selwyn, N., Hillman, T., Bergviken Rensfeldt, A. et al. (2023). Digital Technologies and the Automation of Education — Key Questions and Concerns. *Postdigital Science and Education*, 5, 15–24 (2023). https://doi.org/10.1007/s42438-021-00263-3

Wilton, L., Ip, S., Sharma, M., Fan, F. (2022). Where Is the AI? AI Literacy for Educators. In: Rodrigo, M.M., Matsuda, N., Cristea, A.I., Dimitrova, V. (eds.), *Artificial Intelligence in Education. Posters and Late Breaking Results, Workshops and Tutorials, Industry and Innovation Tracks, Practitioners' and Doctoral Consortium. AIED 2022. Lecture Notes in Computer Science*, vol. 13356. Springer, Cham. https://doi.org/10.1007/978-3-031-11647-6_31

Acknowledgements In the spirit of academic transparency, the authors acknowledges that generative artificial intelligence was employed for the specific and circumscribed purpose of assisting in the translation of this book from Italian to English. This process is best described as AI-assisted translation, where the author directed, reviewed, and revised all generated outputs to ensure the fidelity and nuance of the final text. It must be emphasised that these tools had no role in the ideation, research, structuring of arguments, or the original composition of the work, which remain the sole intellectual contribution of the authors.

Competing Interests The authors have no competing interests to declare that are relevant to the content of this manuscript.

Contents

List of Tables

The Dimensions of Artificial Intelligence Literacy: A Pedagogical Perspective

Abstract This chapter establishes the pedagogical foundation for Artificial Intelligence Literacy (AIL). It begins by addressing the inherent difficulty in defining Artificial Intelligence (AI), reviewing a range of historical definitions from computer science alongside more recent ones from international bodies like the OECD and UNESCO. Adopting a multidimensional perspective, this chapter then introduces its core contribution: a comprehensive pedagogical framework for "critical AI literacy." This framework is structured around four key dimensions: cognitive (knowing AI), operational (using AI), critical (evaluating AI), and ethical (understanding AI's implications). To further contextualise the framework, this chapter clarifies the crucial distinction between AIL (teaching *about* AI) and AI in Education (AIED) (teaching *with* AI). Finally, it examines the ongoing debate on how AIL should be taught, weighing technical versus inclusive approaches, and ultimately advocates for an inclusive, non-specialist model. This approach aims to integrate AIL into school curricula from an early age, fostering the development of informed and critical citizenship in a society increasingly mediated by technology.

Keywords Definitions of A · Artificial Intelligence Literacy (AIL) · AI in Education (AIED) vs AIL · Pedagogical framework · Digital citizenship

M. Ranieri et al., *Artificial Intelligence in Schools*, Digital Education and Learning, https://doi.org/10.1007/978-3-032-15919-9_1

1 Artificial Intelligence: What Definition?

Before the advent of the personal computer, it was commonplace to refer to calculators as "electronic brains"—a term documented in the *Oxford English Dictionary* whose earliest recorded use dates back to the 1940s. In parallel, during the 1960s and 1970s, the term "brain" also gained traction in the media. Comparing these new machines—filled with mysterious electronic circuits rather than familiar gears—to the human brain and attributing to them cognitive capabilities similar to those of intelligent beings was not merely a feature of burgeoning science fiction (consider HAL 9000 in Kubrick's 1968 film *2001: A Space Odyssey*), but also a research perspective pursued by numerous scientists.

As we shall see in chapter "The Cognitive Dimension: Historical Framework and Basic Concepts", the term *Artificial Intelligence* (AI) has existed since the early years of computer science. Yet despite this longevity—and its current ubiquity across numerous contexts—its definition has never been, and still is not, unambiguous, either terminologically or semantically.

This difficulty stems from a nearly century-long history that, particularly from the 1960s onwards, saw scholars and scientists from diverse disciplinary backgrounds attempting to measure the capacity to simulate, generate, and reproduce human intelligence through artificial means. Each discipline—from computer science to psychology, from philosophy to neuroscience—has contributed and continues to contribute its own piece to the puzzle, enriching the field but also complicating the task of providing a simple, straightforward, and universally accepted definition.

Rather than assuming a single definition, let us first examine some of the principal ones, without any claim to exhaustiveness, so that different perspectives and their nuances can be appreciated.

Historically, the invention of the term and the establishment of AI as an autonomous field of research can be traced to McCarthy, who coined the expression in 1955. For McCarthy, AI rested on the conjecture that every aspect of learning and intelligence could, in principle, be described with sufficient precision that a properly designed machine would be able to emulate it (see Sect. 1.1 in chapter "The Cognitive Dimension: Historical Framework and Basic Concepts"). To investigate the potential of this nascent discipline, he organised a seminar with ten of the most distinguished mathematicians and engineers of the time.

A starting point for approaching the issue is to look at the definitions provided by computer science experts—including, alongside the aforementioned McCarthy, the authors of the principal reference text in the field:

- "It is science that is concerned with making machines do things that would require intelligence if done by men" (Minsky, 1968, p. v).
- "It is the study of how to make computers do things at which, at the moment, people are better" (Rich and Knight, 1991, p. xxii).
- "It is the science and engineering of making intelligent machines, especially intelligent computer programs" (McCarthy, 2007, p. i).
- "It is the study of agents that receive percepts from the environment and perform actions. Each such agent implements a function that maps percepts to actions" (Russell and Norvig, 2009, p. viii).
- "It is that activity devoted to making machines intelligent, and intelligence is that quality that enables an entity to function appropriately and with foresight in its environment" (Nilsson, 2010, p. xiii).
- "Our intelligence is what makes us human, and AI is an extension of that quality" (attributed to Yann LeCun, 2018 winner of the Turing Award—the highest honour for AI studies).

These definitions, like many others, explicitly reference human intelligence—without which it seems impossible to clarify what is meant by AI—but we will return to this issue in the next chapter. For now, it is important to note that comparison with human intelligence constitutes a recurring and constitutive element of AI definitions formulated within the technological sphere.

Alongside the definitions of technologists and scientists, as AI applications have become increasingly pervasive and impactful on society, international bodies and agencies have also grappled in recent years with the challenging task of defining this technology. The Organisation for Economic Co-operation and Development (OECD), for example, describes AI as "a set of machine-based systems that can, for a given set of human-defined objectives, make predictions, recommendations or decisions influencing real or virtual environments. AI systems are designed to operate with varying levels of autonomy" (OECD, 2019, p. ii), emphasising the presence of varying degrees of autonomy with which AI applications can operate. This view is expanded by the European Commission's expert group, for whom AI is "a systems that display intelligent behaviour by analysing their environment and taking actions – with some degree of autonomy – to achieve specific goals" (EU, 2018, p. ix). Similarly, the European Parliament emphasises AI's ability to manifest intelligent behaviour by "analysing its environment and taking actions - with some degree of autonomy - to achieve specific goals" (European Parliament, 2018, p. i). It is further specified that AI-based systems can be immaterial (i.e., software-based, acting in the virtual world, such as voice assistants) or embedded in hardware devices (such as advanced robots or autonomous cars). The pervasiveness of this technology and, more recently, its characteristic reliance on enormous amounts of data (see Chapters "The Cognitive Dimension: Historical Framework and Basic Concepts" and The Operational Dimension: Uses and Applications) also raise ethical concerns. For this reason, UNESCO (2021), in its recommendations on AI ethics, emphasises the ability of systems to process information through models and algorithms by which they can learn and handle cognitive tasks, as well as make predictions and decisions in both real and virtual environments.

All the definitions mentioned capture one or more aspects that have characterised the past and present of AI research and debate. Privileging any single one risks being misleading about the complexity of the topic. Nonetheless, with this *caveat* in mind, we adopt the UNESCO (2021) definition, which encompasses a plurality of dimensions: the informational ("processing information through models and algorithms"), the cognitive ("learning and managing cognitive tasks as well as making predictions"), and decision-making ("making decisions in both real and virtual environments"), thereby capturing the multidimensional nature of the construct. As we shall see in the following section, this multidimensional view of AI is reflected in the equally multidimensional articulation of the framework for Artificial Intelligence Literacy, or critical AI literacy, that underpins this volume.

2 A Framework for Artificial Intelligence Literacy

The development of AI is distinguished from previous technological innovations by its extremely rapid evolution, which makes new and increasingly sophisticated applications available within very short time-frames. Within this context, the importance and urgency of a structured framework for understanding AI becomes evident, and in educational terms, there is a clear need for a framework that can enable the development of AI literacy (AIL) or, in the lexicon of this volume, critical AI literacy (Cuomo et al., 2022; Veldhuis et al., 2025).

This imperative is linked, on one hand, to the need to prevent digital divides and social exclusion, and to stem the problems of inequality associated with them, which may in turn raise ideological and socio-political issues (Selwyn, 2023). On the other hand, the need for AI pedagogy (Steinbauer et al., 2021) arises within a scenario of great complexity, as it requires interdisciplinary skills ranging from technical knowledge to mastery of the most appropriate teaching methods to help people understand the theoretical and technological underpinnings of new media, together with their cultural and social dimensions.

Given the variety of domains and applications that now characterise recent AI developments, it is clear that a superficial or fragmented approach to critical AI literacy education is insufficient. Hence the need to rely on a theoretical framework that can conceptualise critical AI literacy holistically and guide individuals and institutions through its many facets.

So, what do we mean by AIL or critical AI literacy?

In the literature, this expression was first proposed in 2016 by Burgsteiner and Kandlhofer, who defined AIL as "the ability to understand the underlying knowledge and concepts of the technologies on which artificial intelligence is based" (Burgsteiner et al., 2016, p. 1; see also Kandlhofer et al., 2016, p. 2). Another prominent definition is that of Druga et al. (2022), who state that AI literacy can be defined as knowledge and understanding of the basic functions of AI and how to use AI applications in everyday life in an ethical way. AI skills include the ability to read, work with, analyse, and create with AI.

Building on these foundations and reiterating the relevance of ethical aspects, other authors add that AIL embraces a set of skills that enable effective and critical communication and collaboration with AI technologies (Long and Magerko, 2020), emphasising the ethical nature of such interactions. Additionally, Ng et al. (2021) included AIL in the list of new media and digital literacies needed for living in the twenty-first century.

From a comparative analysis of these definitions, certain dominant elements emerge which -following and reformulating the articulation proposed by Ng et al. (2021)—can be traced back to four constituent dimensions of the conceptual framework proposed here: the **cognitive dimension** (knowing and understanding AI), the **operational dimension** (using and applying AI), the **critical dimension** (evaluating and creating AI), and, finally, the **ethical dimension** (understanding the ethical implications of AI).

These dimensions not only represent the constituent components of the framework presented here but also provide the conceptual basis for the very structure of this volume, in which each subsequent chapter focuses on a specific dimension. Let us now examine what is meant by each of these dimensions, beginning with the first.

The **cognitive dimension** refers to knowing and understanding AI and concerns the comprehension of fundamental AI concepts, focusing on basic notions and skills that do not require prior technological knowledge (Ng et al., 2021). It is emphasised, for example, that people should not be limited to passive use of AI applications but should be encouraged to understand their operating principles and underlying technologies (Burgsteiner et al., 2016; Kandlhofer et al., 2016), with a view to facilitating approaches to AI-based learning tools and enabling greater insight into associated problems. Furthermore, in line with Su and Zhong (2022), we can articulate knowledge in this area more analytically with reference to the following aspects: (i) "definitions and types of AI," which refers to understanding AI types (i.e., weak/strong) and their underlying technologies; (ii) "data and machine learning," which indicates understanding of the conceptual foundations of machine learning; and (iii) "applications," which concerns knowledge of AI's various application domains.

The second component of the framework concerns the **operational dimension**—that is, knowing how to use and apply AI. This relates to the application of AI concepts and tools in different contexts (Druga et al., 2019; Lee et al., 2021). In this regard, authors such as Vazhayil et al. (2019) point out the importance of designing and implementing algorithms to support learners' understanding of how to use knowledge bases for problem-solving. Also attributed to the operational dimension, in its more advanced stages, are the ability to solve problems using AI tools and the ability to build AI applications with the aim of fostering analytical abstraction (Kim et al., 2021).

The third dimension involves a **critical approach** towards AI use in various application areas, engaging students in cognitive, creative, and critical discernment activities (Su and Zhong, 2022). Beyond popularising AI knowledge and use through concepts and practical examples, AIL is understood to include the ability to consciously and effectively communicate and collaborate with AI technologies, critically evaluate them, and even create artefacts based on them (Long and Magerko, 2020). Moreover, as AI plays an important role in multiple decision-making processes, the ability to critically evaluate the impact associated with its use is essential for enabling deeper understanding of the implications of its various applications. This allows not only for thorough comprehension of AI's underlying dynamics but also for recognising and balancing its positive and negative impacts on society, thereby promoting a more thoughtful approach.

The final component relates to the **ethical dimension**, which concerns the ability to use AI responsibly and consciously. This dimension involves adopting a balanced view of the sensitive ethical issues it raises, such as the possibility of delegating to a machine, wholly or partially, decisions that may significantly impact an individual's personal sphere (e.g., job allocation or the identification of therapeutic pathways). Particularly as AI becomes more widespread and increasingly pervasive in everyday life, there is growing interest in what is termed AI Ethics (Boddington, 2023)—the set of practices aimed at increasing awareness of AI-related risks. Specifically, attention is drawn to the importance of AI that is transparent in its processes and attentive to fairness, accountability, privacy, and security.

The following figure (Fig. 1) schematically represents the dimensions of AIL for implementing critical literacy pathways.

A final observation is in order. The framework should not be viewed as a static instrument that fixes once and for all the conceptual components of AI literacy, thereby turning a living practice into an abstract construct detached from users' engagements. Rather, its function is explicitly pragmatic and orientational. It is intended as a navigational tool to guide educators and teachers in the difficult task of selecting relevant topics to address and competencies to promote, while also facilitating alignment with current curricular approaches.

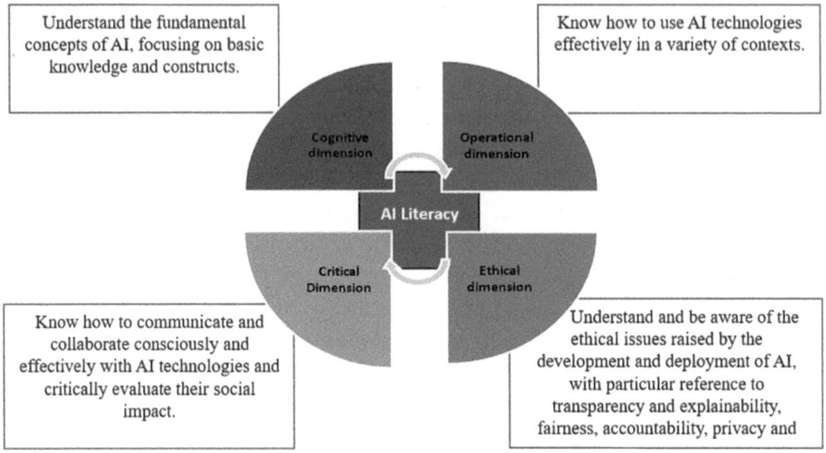

Fig. 1 The dimensions of the critical AI literacy framework

3 AIL and AIED: What Differences?

The relationship between AI and education can be approached in different ways: while AI can be an object of critical literacy, interest in AI can also concern the instrumental use of this technology to support teaching and learning processes.

In the first case, we speak of AIL, which is precisely about teaching artificial intelligence—that is, equipping students with fundamental knowledge of what AI is, how it works, its ethical implications, and its impact on society. This is an educational process that aims to develop individuals who are aware and informed about AI's growing presence in daily lives and its ethical and social ramifications. AIL therefore represents a concept that transcends simple mechanical understanding of AI. While basic knowledge of algorithms and programming is certainly useful—an aspect subsumed under so-called computational thinking (see Sect. 2.2 in chapter "The Cognitive Dimension: Historical Framework and Basic Concepts")—this is only the tip of the iceberg of what it means to be fully AI literate. The heart of AIL lies in the ability to navigate, understand, and interact critically within the complex AI ecosystem. This ecosystem consists of a vast network of influences and interactions interweaving technology, society, and the individual. Students must therefore not only understand how an algorithm works but also how these algorithms, once implemented, can shape behaviours, influence decisions, and even define cultural norms (Manovich, 2020). This requires critical reflection on AI's social implications: how it can accentuate or mitigate existing biases, monitor and influence large population segments, and potentially threaten privacy. Without sketching apocalyptic scenarios, it is easy to imagine how indiscriminate or malicious use of an ecosystem to which we increasingly entrust our decisions (consider the "blind" trust with which we follow a navigator's directions in unfamiliar places) could pose risks to democracy and social equity (Coeckelbergh, 2025; Jungherr, 2023; Yu, 2020). After all, as highlighted in a 2023 European Parliament publication, if not properly managed, AI could lead to decisions influenced by data on ethnicity, gender, or age in contexts such hiring or dismissal, mortgage approval, or even in criminal proceedings. With the emergence of generative AI technologies (see Sect. 1.1 in chapter "The Cognitive Dimension: Historical Framework and Basic Concepts"), through which a person's features or voice can be reproduced as deepfakes, the line between reality and fiction has become more and more blurred—or, put differently, real and virtual are both modalities for presenting being. It is evident that the ability to discern between fact and misinformation has become crucial, albeit ever more difficult. Students, and more generally all citizens, must therefore be equipped with the necessary skills to navigate this sea of information with awareness, determining whether it is authentic or manipulated and distorted by algorithms of varying intent.

Turning to the second case—the instrumental approach—we refer to AI in Education (AIED), which concerns teaching *with* AI. In AIED, AI technologies are viewed as pedagogical supports to improve and personalise teaching and learning processes. In this sense, AIED primarily proposes using AI as an ally in the educational experience, envisioning new opportunities for personalising learning trajectories. For example, intelligent tutoring systems aim to adapt dynamically to each student's skill level and needs, ensuring more personalised and calibrated learning by analysing student data, tailoring the learning path to their performance, and providing immediate feedback. Personalised educational content recommendation can further enrich the learning experience by presenting students with materials and resources that reflect their interests, and areas of strength or improvement, with the intention of fostering more engaging learning by stimulating curiosity and motivation (Baker et al., 2021). Nonetheless, despite its potential, the instrumental use of AI in education also has limitations. One critical issue relates to privacy, as AI systems may pose risks regarding the collection and processing of students' personal data. Additionally, over-reliance on AI tools can sometimes diminish the importance of human interaction in the educational environment—an essential element for students' socio-emotional development. Another limitation is the possibility that AI, while a promising tool for learning personalisation, may fail to adequately account for the cultural and social context in which learning takes place, resulting in educational programmes that are not fully tailored to each student's specific needs and that may perpetuate stereotypes. We will examine these and other challenges in detail in subsequent chapters.

4 Teaching AIL: When to Start and from Where?

The concept of AIL, although relatively recent, has developed over the years, giving rise to academic debate characterised by multiple, sometimes diametrically opposed positions. The central discussion concerns AIL's true essence: what its nature should be and how it should therefore be promoted and taught in different educational settings. On the one hand, there are scholars who view AIL as an inherently technical field. They argue that to achieve true AI literacy it is essential to have a robust foundation in mathematical, statistical, and computing skills. They also maintain that AIL involves—at least partially—familiarity and competence with the tools and techniques that underlie AI itself (Yang et al., 2025).

Another school of thought, however, argues for a more inclusive interpretation of AIL. These scholars contend that literacy should not be reserved only for those with specialised knowledge but should be made accessible to a much broader audience. According to this view, AIL's main goal should be to provide all citizens, regardless of their technical background, with a clear understanding of AI principles, its potential applications, and its ethical and social repercussions.

A more detailed exploration of technically oriented positions highlights contributions by Ng et al. (2021) and Kong et al. (2021). The framework proposed by Ng et al. (2021) distinguishes between technical and non-technical skills in AIL. Through this categorisation, they implicitly suggest a need for specialised training for those who wish to immerse themselves in AI's more technical aspects. This view is evidenced by their inclusion of complex topics such as deep learning and neural networks among necessary core concepts. Indeed, in their section on basic knowledge for AIL, they refer to Russell and Norvig's (2009) *AI Syllabus*—a work with a deep engineering orientation that requires computer science and mathematical-statistical training for comprehension.

Similarly, Kong et al. (2021) address AIL by incorporating both factual knowledge and technical details in their description. Among these, they emphasise the importance of understanding concepts such as data cleaning (i.e., preparing datasets for machine learning), neural networks, computer vision, deep learning, and more sophisticated AI techniques generally. This depth, while providing a more comprehensive overview, actually creates a barrier for those without solid technical foundations.

A possible solution to this barrier has been outlined by Cetindamar et al. (2022). These authors suggest that AI literacy should not be viewed solely through a sharp division between technical and non-technical skills; rather, they propose that the type of interaction an individual has with AI should also be considered as a distinguishing criterion. Such a perspective introduces the idea that different levels of expertise, including specialised expertise, are required to interact with AI. To exemplify, we might consider the difference between those who use AI for day-to-day purposes and those who work on its development and programming: these are two profoundly different modes of interaction that, as Weber et al. (2023) also underlined, presuppose markedly different skill sets and preparation. AIL, like other competences (e.g., digital competence; Calvani et al., 2012), has a contextual nature—that is, contexts of use influence its definition in terms of the descriptive content that qualifies its components.

Other scholars have opted for more inclusive approaches regarding AIL. Long and Magerko (2020), for example, move away from technical complexity to embrace a concept of literacy aimed at non-experts. They reiterate how it is imperative for citizens to have the skills necessary to use effectively AI tools available online, in their homes and workplaces. This inclusive view is not limited to everyday use of AI-based tools but also extends to the ability to understand and evaluate their associated ethical and social implications.

A similar stance is supported by Druga et al. (2019), who stress the importance of AIL focused on the ability to "to learn about AI systems and to think critically about how this technology impacts their lives" (Druga et al., 2021, p. 194). Finally, Laupichler et al. (2022) contribute to this narrative by arguing that AI knowledge and understanding should not be exclusive. For them, AIL represents the body of knowledge and skills necessary for individuals to participate consciously in debates about AI and to make informed decisions about its use and consequences. These approaches represent a call for democratising AI literacy, emphasising the importance of making it accessible and understandable to all.

Although debate on the curricular placement of AI literacy remains heated—both regarding the disciplines involved and learners' age—the authors' position (Cuomo et al., 2022) is that AI literacy should encompass the associated knowledge and skills within the framework of the basic competences that citizens must possess to exercise their citizenship responsibly and actively.

Indeed, while there are important technical components to understanding AI, they should not, in our opinion, become a reason for excluding large portions of the population from active and informed participation in this crucial field of knowledge and everyday existence. An educational, multidimensional, and inclusive approach to AI that envisages not only technical aspects, but also pedagogically significant dimensions of a critical-cognitive and ethical-social nature appears feasible and sustainable within schools, precisely because of the multidisciplinary and transversal nature of the areas that can potentially be involved. Integrating AIL into school curricula from primary and secondary levels will foster the growth of citizens capable of navigating the digital world with critical competence, ethical awareness, and safety, actively participating in global debates about AI and its role in our societies.

References

Baker R. *et al.* (2021), *Towards sharing student models across learning systems*, in *International Conference on Artificial Intelligence in Education*, Cham, Springer International Publishing, pp. 60–65.

Boddington, P. (2023), *AI Ethics. A Textbook*, Springer Nature, Berlin (1st ed.).

Burgsteiner H., Kandlhofer M., & Steinbauer G. (2016), *IRobot: Teaching the Basics of Artificial Intelligence in High Schools*, in *Proceedings of the AAAI conference on artificial intelligence*, *30*(1), pp.1426–27.

A. Calvani; A.Fini; M. Ranieri; P. Picci (2012). *Are young generations in secondary school digitally competent? A study on Italian teenagers.* COMPUTERS & EDUCATION, vol. 58, pp. 797–807. https://doi.org/10.1016/j.compedu.2011.10.004

Cetindamar D. *et al.* (2022), *Explicating AI Literacy of Employees at Digital Workplaces*, in IEEE Transactions on Engineering Management, pp. 1–14.

Coeckelbergh, M. (2025). LLMs, truth, and democracy: an overview of risks. Science and Engineering Ethics, 31(1), 4..

Cuomo S., Biagini G., Ranieri M. (2022), *Artificial Intelligence Literacy, what it is and how to promote it. From literature analysis to a proposed Framework*, in "Media Education," *13*(2), pp. 161–72.

Druga S. *et al.* (2019), *Inclusive AI literacy for kids around the world*, in Proceedings of FabLearn *2019*, Proceedings of FabLearn, pp. 104–11.

Druga, S., Yip, J., Preston, M., & Dillon, D. (2021). "The 4As: Ask, Adapt, Author, Analyze—AI Literacy Framework for Families."

Druga S., Christoph F. L., Ko A. J. (2022), *Family as a Third Space for AI Literacies: How do children and parents learn about AI together?* in *CHI Conference on Human Factors in Computing Systems* (New Orleans April 30–May 5, 2022), Association for Computing Machinery, New York, NY, pp. 1–17.

European Commission (2018), Communication from the Commission to the European Parliament, the European Council, the Council, the European Economic and Social Committee and the Committee of the Regions. Artificial Intelligence for Europe. https://eur-lex.europa.eu/legal-content/EN/TXT/?uri=COM%3A2018%3A237%3AFIN

Jungherr A. (2023), *Artificial Intelligence and Democracy: A Conceptual Framework*, in "Social Media + Society," 9(3), pp.1–14.

Kandlhofer, M. *et al.* (2016), *Artificial intelligence and computer science in education: From kindergarten to university*, in "IEEE Frontiers in Education Conference (FIE)," 1–9.

Kim S. *et al.* (2021), *Why and What to Teach: AI Curriculum for Elementary School*, in *Proceedings of the AAAI Conference on Artificial Intelligence*, *35*(17), pp. 15569–76.

Kong S.-C., Man-Yin Cheung W., Zhang, G. (2021), *Evaluation of an artificial intelligence literacy course for university students with diverse study backgrounds*, in Computers and Education: Artificial Intelligence, 2, 100026.

Laupichler M.C., *et al.* (2022), *Artificial intelligence literacy in higher and adult education: A scoping literature review*, in Computers and Education: Artificial Intelligence, 3, p. 100101.

Lee I. *et al.* (2021), *Developing Middle School Students' AI Literacy*, Proceedings of the 52nd *ACM Technical Symposium on Computer Science Education*, (SIGCSE 21, March 13–20, 2021, virtual event, USA), Association for Computing Machinery, New York, NY, pp. 191–7.

Long D., Magerko B. (2020), *What is AI Literacy? Competencies and Design Considerations*, in *Proceedings of the 2020 CHI Conference on Human Factors in Computing Systems*, 1–16 (Honolulu April 25–30, 2020), Association for Computing Machinery, New York, NY.

Manovich L. (2020), *Cultural Analytics*. The MIT Press.

McCarthy J. (2007), *What is Artificial Intelligence* (http://www.formal.stanford.edu/jmc/whatisai/whatisai.html).

Minsky M. (1968), *Semantic information processing*, MIT press, Cambridge, MA.

Ng D.T.K. *et al.* (2021), *Conceptualizing AI literacy: An exploratory review*, in Computers and Education: Artificial Intelligence, 2, 100041.

Nilsson N.J. (2010), *The Quest for Artificial Intelligence: A History of Ideas and Achievements*, Cambridge University Press, Cambridge.

OECD (2019), *Recommendation of the Council on Artificial Intelligence*, OECD Publishing, Paris, (https://oecd.ai/en/assets/files/OECD-LEGAL-0449-en.pdf).

Rich E., Knight K. (1991), *Artificial Intelligence*, McGraw-Hill, New York, NY.

Russell S. J., Norvig P. (2009), *Artificial intelligence: a modern approach*, Prentice Hall, Upper Saddle River, NJ.

Selwyn N. *et al.* (2023), *Digital Technologies and the Automation of Education - Key Questions and Concerns* in "Postdigit Sci Educ," 5, pp. 15–24.

Steinbauer G., *et al.* (2021), *A Differentiated Discussion About AI Education K-12*, in "KI - Künstliche Intelligenz," 35(2), pp. 131–7.

Su J., Zhong Y. (2022), *Artificial Intelligence (AI) in early childhood education: Curriculum design and future directions*, in Computers and Education: Artificial Intelligence, 3, 100072.

UNESCO (2021). *AI and Education: Guidance for Policymakers*, (https://unesdoc.unesco.org/ark: /48223/pf0000376709).

Vazhayil A. *et al.* (2019), *Focusing on Teacher Education to Introduce AI in Schools: Perspectives and Illustrative Findings*, in *IEEE Tenth International Conference on Technology for Education (T4E)* (India, December 10–13, 2018), IEEE, New York, NY, pp. 71–7.

Veldhuis, A., Lo, P. Y., Kenny, S., & Antle, A. N. (2025). *Critical artificial intelligence literacy: A scoping review and framework synthesis.* International Journal of Child-Computer Interaction, 43, 100708. https://doi.org/10.1016/j.ijcci.2024.100708

Weber P., Pinski M., Baum, L. (2023), *Toward an Objective Measurement of AI Literacy.* (https://aisel.aisnet.org/pacis2023/60/).

Yang, Y., Zhang, Y., Sun, D., He, W., & Wei, Y. (2025). *Navigating the landscape of AI literacy education: insights from a decade of research* (2014–2024). Humanities and Social Sciences Communications, 12, 374. https://doi.org/10.1057/s41599-025-04583-8

Yu P. K. (2020), *The Algorithmic Divide and Equality in the Age of Artificial Intelligence*, in Florida Law Review, 72(2), pp. 331–90.

The Cognitive Dimension: Historical Background and Key Concepts

Abstract This chapter explores the cognitive dimension of Artificial Intelligence Literacy by tracing the historical and conceptual evolution of "automatic thinking." It begins with a historical overview, charting the human aspiration to create intelligent automata—from ancient myths and mechanical contraptions such as the Mechanical Turk to the development of logical-computational machines by pioneers such as Babbage and Lovelace. The narrative then pivots to the modern era, explaining the significance of the Turing Test and detailing the foundational split between Symbolic AI (rule-based systems) and Subsymbolic AI (machine learning). After establishing this historical context, this chapter examines the pervasive, "onlife" reality of AI in the lives of children and adolescents, arguing that traditional approaches of technological prohibition are no longer viable. In response, two pedagogical methods are proposed to foster a foundational understanding of AI. The first is *Philosophy for Children (P4C)*, a maieutic approach to critically discuss the complex nature of intelligence itself. The second is the teaching of *computational thinking*, using practical methods like unplugged coding to demystify the algorithmic processes that underpin AI's "intelligent behaviour."

Keywords History of AI · Turing Test · Symbolic AI · Subsymbolic AI · Computational thinking · Philosophy for Children (P4C)

M. Ranieri et al., *Artificial Intelligence in Schools*, Digital Education and Learning, https://doi.org/10.1007/978-3-032-15919-9_2

1 Themes and Issues

1.1 From Automata to Artificial Intelligence: A Brief History of "Automatic Thinking"

Since ancient times, one of humanity's foremost aspirations has been to create life from inanimate matter. While bringing forth life from life is prerogative of all living beings, animating the inanimate has been reserved for the gods. Fashioning an intelligent creature able to communicate with its creator, loyal to that creator's will, and endowed with capacities approaching invincibility and immortality, would render humans god-like. Unsurprisingly, myths of humankind formed from clay recur across cultures, from the Hebrew narrative to the legend of Prometheus and to Chinese cosmogonies.

The presence of automata (from the Greek αὐτόματος, meaning "that which is able to move itself")—that is, human-made figures that behave as if alive—permeates all Western literature. Beginning with the myth of Talos (Mayor, 2018), the invincible bronze automaton that Zeus gives to Minos to guard the island of Crete, tales of artificial beings recur across the centuries: from Ovid's *Metamorphoses* and medieval legends, to the Golem of Hebrew literature, E.T.A. Hoffmann's *Nutcracker*, and Mary Shelley's famous *Frankenstein*, not to mention Mel Brooks' parodic yet perceptive film *Young Frankenstein* (1974). Children's literature is equally rich in stories about automatons. *Pinocchio*, *The Wizard of Oz*, Andersen's "*The Steadfast Tin Soldier*," and the ballets *Coppélia* and *The Nutcracker* all feature inanimate characters endowed with human traits.

In the twentieth century, the term "automaton" gave way to "robot" (from the Czech *robota*, meaning "forced labour") within science-fiction literature, which since the middle of the last century has generated a vast corpus of novels and films. Prominent examples include Isaac Asimov's collection, *I, Robot*, which inspired Proyas' eponymous movie (2004), and Philip K. Dick's novel *Do Androids Dream of Electric Sheep?* (1968), adapted by Ridley Scott as *Blade Runner* (1982). The latter work raises enduring fascinating questions of ethical nature about technologies that, pushed to extremes, produce androids indistinguishable from human beings—capable even of emotion and self-questioning.

Beyond literature, historical evidence of functional automata dates back to antiquity. The earliest recorded device is the Philo's Automatic Servant (third century BCE): when a cup was placed in its left hand, the right arm, holding a pitcher, automatically raised and poured a preset mixture of water and wine. Similar inventions appeared in later centuries, culminating in the nineteenth century, when an automaton was first presented that purported not only to move but also to "think" like a human being.

In 1769, inventor von Kempelen unveiled the *Mechanical Turk* (Standage, 2002) to fashionable society—a machine said to play, and even win, at chess. The automaton had the appearance of a Turk, dressing contemporary Middle Eastern garb. It was connected to a large cabinet packed with gears enabling its movements. Presented to Empress Maria Theresa and her court, the Turk amazed onlookers not only with its chess prowess but also with its ability to write responses in several languages on a slate, drawing also the attention of various scientists of the day. In short, the Turk generated excitement, interest, and questions in both society and the scientific community of the time until, several decades later, it was exposed as .... a hoax! The cabinet, purportedly crammed with gears, actually concealed the hiding place of a human chess player who, via hidden levers, moved the pieces and communicated with the public.

Yet, although it was an illusion, the Mechanical Turk marks a seminal moment in the history of Artificial Intelligence (AI), because for the first time humans were confronted with a machine that convincingly simulated human behaviour. Disappointment at the revelation of the Turk's real nature dampened enthusiasm, but the growing demands imposed by the industrial revolution made the need to automate not only movements but also skills most closely related to mental labour—particularly computation, which until then had been done manually without any mechanical aid (Raugh and Probst, 2019)—increasingly pressing.

From the mid-seventeenth century onwards, mechanical automata were complemented by what might be called logical automata, designed to relieve humans of the burden of manual calculation (Swade, 2022). The first known calculator, built in 1623 by the German Wilhelm Schickard for the astronomer Kepler, could perform the four basic operations. Just over twenty years later, the philosopher Blaise Pascal produced the Pascaline, a machine to perform arithmetic calculations. The eighteenth century witnessed further advances in automatic calculating devices, although accuracy limitations continued to hamper their practical use.

To overcome these limitations, around 1830, Charles Babbage—a mathematician and educator—designed a calculating tool known as the *Difference Engine* (Swade, 2000), intended to generate the numerical tables required for complex computations. The machine's design was extremely complex: once completed, it would have measured roughly two metres wide and two-and-a-half metres tall. Due to its complexity, it never came to fruition except for a reduced version made in 1832. Its peculiarity was that an operator could use the device without understanding its underlying principles, so much so that some contemporary scientists remarked that it was "the marvellous pulp and fibre of a brain had been substituted by brass and iron" (ivi, p. 85), calling it a true "thinking machine" (ibid.).

Babbage continued his research by designing a far more ambitious device, the *Analytical Engine*, regarded as the first conception of a modern computer. Planned to be controlled by punched cards, it was meant to perform general calculations rather than produce fixed tables. Although never constructed, it stands as the earliest design for a universal, programmable machine. Here, it is worth mentioning the fundamental role of Lady Lovelace, the daughter of the poet Byron: she was one of the few who grasped the potential of the Analytical Engine and often cited as the first computer programmer in history, having devised a procedure to compute Bernoulli numbers.

Despite these insights, the realisation of a machine capable of imitating human reasoning stalled because of technical complexity. To acknowledge substantial progress, one must wait until the first half of the twentieth century, when nascent electronics through transistors—particularly solid-state transistors—made it feasible to build circuits that operated at very high speeds without the tolerances and mechanical stresses—intrinsic to any mechanical device—that hampered Babbage's designs.

The distinguishing feature of these circuits, defined as digital, was that they worked exclusively with two states, or bits: HIGH and LOW voltage. Whereas earlier mechanical calculating machines were designed to run with gears in which each click was linked to a digit between 0 and 9, digital machines instead operate with only two bits that can be associated with the symbols 0 (zero) and 1.

In addition to enabling mathematical calculations as the traditional decimal system, the binary system can also implement logic, interpreting HIGH as **TRUE** and LOW as **FALSE**, thereby enabling computers—when properly programmed—to make decisions based on the logical values (TRUE/FALSE) presented to it. Therefore, any binary system possesses the feature, theorised in the mid-nineteenth century by the English mathematician and logician Boole, of being able to operate with both numbers and logical symbols. This property underpins today's entire digital ecosystem, from general-purpose computers to embedded electronics and artificial intelligence systems (Warwick, 2012).

The development of computers in the middle of the last century initiated enormous and extremely rapid technological progress, since for the first time in history humans were able to build a machine capable of performing two activities—numerical calculation and logical reasoning—that distinguish human intelligence. It was therefore natural to wonder whether, at least in theory, a computer could be intelligent—that is, whether humans would ever succeed in fulfilling their ancient dream of creating something thinking from inanimate matter: an artificial intelligence.

Speculations about a machine's ability to simulate intelligent behaviour dates back to the earliest days of computer science, particularly with Turing's work. In 1950, Turing's seminal work *Computing Machinery and Intelligence*, explicitly addressed the issue of whether a computer could be intelligent with the famous question: Can machines think? Fully aware of the difficulty of defining thinking in relation to a machine, Turing proposed that a system could be regarded as intelligent if it passed what later became known as the Turing Test (Turing, 1950).

In the test, an impartial (human) judge communicates—say, via keyboard—with both a human and a machine; if the judge cannot tell which is which, the machine is said to have passed. Turing thus shifted attention away from pinning down a formal definition of artificial intelligence (see Sect. 1.1 in chapter "The Dimensions of Artificial Intelligence Literacy: A Pedagogical Perspective") and towards a machine's capacity to imitate human thought. Appropriately, the section in which he introduces the test is entitled "*The Imitation Game*" a title later adopted for the 2014 film about his life. Following this functional criterion, a machine is intelligent when it is able to respond as a human might. If we play chess with our smartphone, it serves as a capable opponent, and if we want to be guided to reach an unknown destination, a satellite-navigation system can guide us more efficiently than a passenger consulting a paper map. In both cases, the machine displays intelligent behaviour: it selects the best chess move or plots the quickest route on the basis of real-time data.

The AI underpinning such systems is often called symbolic AI (Boden, 2016) because it is based on symbols and logical rules that mirror aspects of human reasoning. Symbolic approaches dominated until a few years ago and produced increasingly refined applications such as modern GPS software that, by exploiting real-time traffic information, may recommend a longer path that nevertheless reduces overall travel time. These systems, however, face two main limitations. First, they are single purpose, i.e., they are aimed at specific tasks (it is difficult to play chess with a satellite navigator!). Second, improvements can only be achieved by rewriting or extending the code; beyond a certain complexity, it becomes impractical to supply a machine with explicit rules for every possible situation.

To address these limitations, a parallel branch of AI, often called subsymbolic AI, has developed which adopts a different approach. Instead of programming the machine to deal with every possible aspect of a scenario, the machine itself learns appropriate behaviour from data. This paradigm relies on neural networks, a foundational concept of AI, that underpins modern Machine Learning (ML).

Neural networks were first formalised by McCulloch and Pitts as early as 1943, with a mathematical model inspired by biological neurons. Just as in the human brain biological neurons are interconnected and react to electrical discharges by propagating them to other neurons, so in artificial neural networks (Gurney, 1997) the aforementioned binary signals (HIGH and LOW) are used to send them to a network of artificial neurons—actually blocks of instructions—that interact with each other. When properly programmed, such a system can acquire capabilities autonomously. To achieve it, the machine is trained to recognise the output by providing it with a set of data and criteria for whether the result is correct. Suppose examples of squares are given to the system as the training set, along with criteria that tell the machine whether the classification performed is correct. If the network makes a mistake in classifying a shape (e.g., categorising it as a "square" when it is actually a triangle), the error signal adjusts internal coefficients until sufficient accuracy is reached.

At the end, the network is able to automatically classify the "squares," exhibiting inductive behaviour; that is, after a correct training it can, in principle, extend the classification to all square shapes. In a sense, we can say that it has learned, automatically, the concept of "square."

A typical application of ML is automatic handwriting recognition. Letters are encoded by certain visual features (e.g., an "n" has two vertical strokes, while an "m" three), enabling the neural network to correctly classify handwriting it has never encountered before. As is easy to imagine, neural networks, partly because of their analogy with the functioning of biological neurons, aroused enormous interest when they were presented. Despite this, practical applications had a troubled existence (Minsky and

Papert, 1968), because accuracy depends heavily on the amount of data with which the network is trained (e.g., many people write an "n" in a "u"-like manner). Moreover, since the learning process is computationally intensive, it requires much more powerful machines than those available in the middle of the last century.

Neural networks and machine learning research generally experienced long periods of low interest—the so-called "AI winters" between the 1970s and 1980s and then in the 1990s. During this time, efforts focused on symbolic AI, particularly on expert systems (Feigenbaum and Feldman, 1963) capable of solving specific problems, such as in medicine or finance, based on human knowledge accumulated in that field and provided to the machine. These applications belong to Weak Artificial Intelligence or, according to other terminologies, Narrow Artificial Intelligence, because they are able to imitate human intelligence but only within specific areas.

The recent renaissance of machine learning systems can be attributed to two main factors. First, modern computers offer vastly greater computational and storage capacity, millions of times higher than their 1980s counterparts. Second, and even more important, is the unprecedented availability of data (see also Chapters "The Operational Dimension: Uses and Applications" and "The Critical Dimension: Understanding and Evaluation Beyond Automation"). In the 1980s, data to train a neural network mostly had to be collected on an ad hoc basis, which inevitably led to a limited and often insufficient amount of data for adequate training. Since the 2000s, however, the growth of the Internet and social media has enabled the emergence of what Floridi (2014) calls the *infosphere*: an environment in which information is ubiquitous and interconnected, and in which every user acts as a *prosumer*—simultaneously producing (e.g., by posting a photograph) and consuming (e.g., by browsing a webpage) data.

Based on it, while until a few years ago training AI for face-recognition relied on modest image archives, now simply scrolling through a Facebook or Instagram page exposes models to millions, perhaps billions, of faces. The main contribution to the development of the infosphere comes from the *Internet of Things*, in which most objects around us, even the most mundane ones, communicate with the Internet and, in principle, make available enormous amounts of data, even of a very sensitive nature, about our lives and behaviours.

A smartwatch can communicate data about our heart rate or physical activity, while supermarket loyalty cards keep track of our eating habits and preferences. All of this, multiplied across a large part of the world's population and for every moment of the day, produces an unimaginable volume of sensitive data whose use poses significant problems, as will be explained in the next chapters.

Beyond these considerations, the virtually unlimited availability of data has provided new and unstoppable impetus for subsymbolic AI, so much so that since 2010, Deep Learning (DL) has emerged as a dominant branch of ML (LeCun et al., 2015). In deep learning, models learn even more autonomously, automatically extracting both explicit and latent features from raw data with minimal human intervention. Whereas traditional ML approaches to handwriting recognition required human intervention defining the characteristics (features) of each individual letter, DL systems infer those features directly—for example, distinguishing "n" from "m"—and can even learn orthographic constraints, such as the rule in English that the prefix *in-* becomes *im-* before words starting with *m* or *p*, as in *impossible* or *immature*.

Although artificial intelligence had been progressing for years, the breakthrough that propelled it into mainstream awareness came around 2014 with the emergence of Generative Artificial Intelligence (GAI) (Goodfellow et al., 2014). Based on sophisticated mathematical theories, this branch of AI not only supports specific problem-solving activities but also the creation of objects not previously resident in the computer's memory. If a DL algorithm can identify one face among thousands, GAI can generate a new artificial face that cannot be distinguished from a human being's picture. A major factor behind GAI's continuing success is its new accessibility to non-experts: tools like DALL-E and Midjourney let anyone create photorealistic or artistic images, while the now-famous ChatGPT enables users to generate coherent, natural-sounding text that is virtually indistinguishable from human writing. The GAI's generativity has, of course, several pedagogical implications that are crucial also for AI literacy and will be discussed in chapter "The Critical Dimension: Understanding and Evaluation Beyond Automation".

In light of these recent, and partly unforeseen, advancements can we legitimately contend that the machine now satisfies the criteria of the Turing Test, that its behavioural outputs are indistinguishable from those of a human interlocutor, and that artificial intelligence has effectively prevailed in the imitation game? At present, the issue remains contested among scholars, and no definitive consensus has been reached. Although particular systems have satisfied the Turing Test under limited dimensions of human–computer interaction, no artificial intelligence has yet achieved a full, unequivocal pass across all evaluative criteria. Despite the remarkable speed of recent advances, it remains impossible to determine whether so-called Strong Artificial Intelligence—capable not merely of imitating behaviour but of displaying human traits such as emotionality and empathy—will materialise in the near future, or whether machines will always remain circumscribed by their mechanistic foundations (Mitchell, 2020; Landers, 2025). The question, still keenly disputed, has moved far beyond the technical sphere and now engages scholars across philosophy, neuroscience, sociology, pedagogy, and other disciplines.

1.2 Children in the Age of Digital Technologies and AI

Digital technologies are now woven into the fabric of everyday life in industrialised nations. By 2017, mobile-phone subscriptions in OECD member states already exceeded their total populations (Burns and Gottschalk, 2020), and according to the latest ITU report, 79% of the global population aged 15–24 uses the Internet—13 percentage points more than the rest of the population—peaking at 99% in high-income countries (ITU, 2024).

The relationship between digital technologies and children has always been a subject of study (to mention just a few works, see Bolshaw and Josephidou, 2023; Buckingham, 2013; Livingstone and Bovill, 2013; Blum-Ross et al., 2018; Postman, 1982), also from an educational perspective (Hobbs, 2021; Ranieri, 2019), especially since age itself appears to present no obstacle to using digital machines. On the contrary, according to some studies (Mascheroni and Siibak, 2021), first contacts with digital media occur between the first and second year of life, even before learning to speak or walk. Children likewise master screen-based gestures—tapping, swiping, pinching to zoom—largely on their own, employing them to navigate favourite apps and thereby cultivating a pronounced familiarity with digital technology. Such pervasiveness and precocity have sparked extensive debate among scholars and educators about the opportunities and risks of exposing young children to digital media. Particularly noteworthy is the critical stance adopted by French psychiatrist Tisseron (2013), who advises against exposing toddlers to digital technologies and recommends their gradual introduction only up to the age of 12.

During the decade since Tisseron's study, digital technologies have progressively permeated every aspect of daily life. As Knox (2019) observes, in the current post digital condition, digital technologies are no longer separable from everyday human practices; they are deeply entangled within social, political, and economic systems, rendering obsolete any attempt to delineate their boundaries. This view is summarised by Floridi, who as early as 2015 coined the expression *onlife,* a contraction of "online" and "life" to indicate a society (ours) where "it is no longer sensible to ask whether one may be online or offline" (ibid., p. 1), because there is no longer a clear and obvious boundary between human and machine, between real and digital.

In this technological scenario, AI has brought about a further change, where perspectives centred on banning or gradually phasing technology into children's lives are likely to be more difficult to pursue. For example, whereas devices such as smartphones or video-game consoles readily lend themselves to guidelines like "keep children from using smartphones" or "restrict time spent on video games," can equally clear prescriptions be formulated for artificial intelligence? Put differently, and adapting Tisseron's logic, what practical meaning might a guideline have that urges postponing children's exposure to AI until a specified age or, alternatively, curbing their engagement with it to some "acceptable" threshold? The answer to this question is really complex and must take into account, on one hand, the levels of ubiquity that digital technology has reached and, on the other hand, the need to ensure the harmonious development of children and teens both physically and socially and emotionally.

As we have seen in Sect. 2.1.1, the infosphere constitutes an environment which, like the atmosphere, surrounds us and is saturated with data entered via interactive devices and subsequently processed by AI. When we query a search engine and the results are filtered based on our interests, when our smartwatch gently reminds us that we exercise too little, it means that our data and the data of millions of other users have been processed somewhere remotely and returned in the form of information thanks to AI applications (see Sect. 1.1 in chapter "The Operational Dimension: Uses and Applications").

Consequently, so long as technology is employed, contact with AI remains inescapable. In addition, as interaction with AI—particularly Generative AI—becomes more natural, it demands fewer, basic technical skills, which are not necessarily critical. Only a few years ago, learning where Napoleon died meant booting up a computer, opening a browser, and typing a query into a search engine; now the same information is available simply by plugging in a voice assistant, connecting to Wi-Fi, and asking, “Hey Google, where did Napoleon die?”.

Such ease of use has a downside: when we interact with a system (e.g., a call centre autoresponder), we will never be sure whether the response comes from a human or an AI and, if so, how neutral and objective the response is or whether it is biased by other interests. For example, if we are subscribers to a streaming service, the provider will recommend TV series and films similar to those we have already watched and liked on our home page—what is called a recommendation system—but we cannot actually know how closely these products really match our interests or whether, rather, they are the ones most promoted by the producer. The opacity of AI (see Sect. 1.2 in chapter “The Critical Dimension: Understanding and Evaluation Beyond Automation”), in relation to how it processes data to provide us with results, leads us to address the second issue we have raised—namely, the imperative of overseeing the cognitive and affective development of new generations in this context of accelerated digitisation. Here, we reach the heart of ethical and pedagogical issues.

As an alternative to prohibition-based strategies, which are increasingly difficult to control, we look to media education approaches that cultivate critical awareness and promote shared educational and social responsibility, while still recognising the importance of broader factors related to governance and regulation, which play a fundamental role in this domain. The proposal of critical literacy pathways in the field of AI, as is done through this volume, reflects this imperative and gives substance to the idea of promoting a critical and responsible view on these issues. The implications of this approach will be examined in the forthcoming chapters: chapter “The Critical Dimension: Understanding and Evaluation Beyond Automation” addresses critical understanding, while chapter “The Ethical Dimension: General Principles and Educational Proposals” addresses the ethical and pedagogical dimensions both essential to analysing the relationship between children and AI systems.

Returning to the literature on the relationship between children and technologies, the scholarship on the topic is extensive and nuanced, shifting in emphasis according to context—such as the school setting (Ranieri, 2019) versus the family environment (Page Jeffery, 2025)—and according to disciplinary lens, most notably educational technology (Halder and Saha, 2023) and media education research (Frau-Meigs et al.,

2021). There is also a substantial body of studies examining the relationship between childhood, adolescence, and smart technologies, particularly on the interaction between children and robots. Much work is available on so-called social robots which can interact with humans; perhaps the most famous is the robot Nao, also used for educational activities and in some supportive therapies for autism spectrum disorders (e.g., see Amirova et al., 2021). Notably, this body of research concentrates on children's social and emotional interactions with anthropomorphic or zoomorphic artefacts, exemplified by the robotic dog Aibo. A specific line of research concerns computational thinking and coding, which from Papert onwards has been prominent in the debate on the relationship between children and computers. As well known, in his volume *Mindstorms: Children, Computers, and Powerful Ideas*, first published in 1980, Papert argues that computers are powerful cognitive tools that can help children develop critical-thinking skills, problem-solving abilities, and creativity, as discussed in Sect. 2.2.2 below.

Currently, limited literature is available on the relationship between childhood, adolescence, and AI. This is mainly due to the sudden explosion of very recent generative AI applications that pose not only educational but also cognitive, social, and relational questions (Ameen et al., 2024). While the debate on how to approach ChatGPT from an educational standpoint is already lively (see chapter "The Critical Dimension: Understanding and Evaluation Beyond Automation"), the social and affective implications remain unknown. While the scientific literature is still consolidating initial findings, leading international bodies have already published insightful reports (AI HLEG, 2019; OECD, 2025; UNICEF, 2021), highlighting that with no doubt artificial intelligence will change the way children interact with their surroundings, including the learning, play, and development environment. Of particular note is the European Commission's research report (Charisi et al., 2022), which underscores the pedagogical potential of AI applications while simultaneously focusing on the main risks, including children's exposure to excessive datafication with obvious privacy implications, the lack of transparency and explainability of key commercial applications, and the risk, common to all technologies, of increasing the division between those who have access to technologies and those who are more or less excluded from them (see chapter "The Ethical Dimension: General Principles and Educational Proposals" for further discussion).

In sum, the rising generation needs less guidance on the now-intuitive mechanics of AI interaction and more pedagogical effort devoted to cultivating an informed, critical understanding of applications whose exchanges are so human-like that even experienced users find it increasingly difficult to distinguish machine from person or to judge the authenticity and objectivity of the responses.

2 Methods and Tools

2.1 *Philosophy for Children: A Maieutic Approach to the Discussion of (Artificial) Intelligence*

As we have seen in chapter "The Dimensions of Artificial Intelligence Literacy: A Pedagogical Perspective", most definitions of AI refer to a machine capable of reproducing human intelligence; an educational activity focusing on the cognitive dimension of AI cannot, therefore, be separated from reflection on the nature of intelligence itself.

Although the most systematic studies on the definition of intelligence can be traced back to the second half of the nineteenth century, the concept of intelligence permeates many cultures through the centuries. In the current state of research, the definition or even the very understanding of the concept of intelligence appears to be extremely variable depending on the disciplinary perspective from which it is considered and dependent on the historical, geographical, and cultural context.

While in Western countries the idea of intelligence is predominantly associated with logical-mathematical skills, in Eastern cultures it places greater emphasis on benevolence, humility, and intrapersonal competences—particularly self-knowledge—than on purely cognitive attributes; moreover, in many African cultures it is equated with interpersonal skills (meant as the ability to maintain relationships) (Sternberg, 2000).

With the development of psychology and psychometrics, research has attempted to unify the definition of the construct of intelligence. In one of its special issues, still valid today, the *Journal of Educational Psychology* in 1921 asked leading researchers of the time for a definition of intelligence. The definitions obtained show how absent any common thread seems to be that could group them under one overarching concept, as if intelligence were an inherently multidimensional concept and any definition could be nothing more than partial.

Further studies focused to a greater extent on the measurement of intelligence, analysing particularly logical-deductive and verbal abilities, until, in 1983, Gardner proposed his theory of Multiple Intelligences and, in accordance with this, provided a definition according to which intelligence is "a biopsychological potential to process information" (Gardner, 2009, p. 5). Given the heterogeneous nature of information processed by individuals, Gardner theorises that there is not just one type, but several forms of intelligence, while classic psychometric tests tend to measure only some abilities (particularly logic-mathematics or language) while neglecting others (e.g., kinaesthetic) that are equally vital to human development.

In short, Gardner identifies nine types of intelligence in relation to different abilities:

- **Logical-mathematical**: analyse problems in a logical-deductive way
- **Linguistic-verbal**: learning to reproduce and use language
- **Musical**: distinguish and reproduce musical patterns, tones, and rhythms
- **Visual-spatial**: recognise, organise, and operate in space
- **Bodily-kinesthetic**: using one's body correctly
- **Interpersonal**: empathy towards other people and teamwork
- **Intrapersonal**: being aware of oneself and one's emotions
- **Naturalistic**: understanding and interacting with the environment
- **Existential**: reflecting on one's own existence

Although certain types of intelligence seem tied to sensory capacities, they are, in fact, largely independent of any sensory impairments. Indeed, in his studies, Gardner mentions subjects with visual impairments who were able to reason effectively in spatial terms or subjects with hearing deficits who exhibited marked musical intelligence—which is not surprising given that Beethoven, who suffered from hearing impairment from a young age, composed the Ninth Symphony despite being almost completely deaf.

Despite the criticism that the theory of multiple intelligences has attracted within the scientific community, chiefly because it resists comprehensive, objective measurement, it has met with great favour, particularly in education, as it can provide teachers with a coherent theoretical framework and support for developing learning environments responsive to student diversity (Gardner, 2009).

Notwithstanding its partial and incomplete character, the foregoing discussion highlights the complexity of conceptualising and defining human intelligence. It therefore prompts a further question: what, in this light, should be regarded as artificial—namely, which of the dimensions outlined above, and to what extent, must a machine replicate to qualify as intelligent?

In order to promote independent reflection in students on the concept of intelligence, both human and artificial, the Philosophy for Children (P4C) approach, conceived by philosopher M. Lipman in 1976, is highly appropriate. According to P4C, there is no lower age limit for posing philosophical questions to children, but adequate preparation is also required in terms of personal skills and proposed materials. P4C exhibits clear affinities with Dewey's pedagogy and Inquiry-Based Learning and adopts a Socratic-maieutic model where the teacher abandons a transmission-of-knowledge stance to become a facilitator—indeed, an intentional "complicator" who foregrounds the topic's critical aspects—so as to stimulate peer dialogue.

Although P4C over the years has been structured into a body of practices and recommendations, the basic principles are easily applicable. Once the problem under investigation has been clarified, concise and simple stimuli (e.g., a short text, a work of art, a film clip) can be introduced to spark dialogue and keep attention centred on the issue at hand. Evidently, the approach can be applied effectively across developmental stages—from primary education onwards—by tailoring the materials and the depth of discussion. Even the teaching methods to implement it can be different according to pupils' age. For instance, circle time can be used in primary school, while digital tools such as Padlet can support the learning activities with older students. In any case, the teacher's role is not to steer the discussion towards consensus; instead, it is to keep uncertainties and alternative possibilities in view, thus heightening students' awareness of the topic's inherent complexity.

A prior examination of the notion of intelligence is indispensable to any cognitive analysis of AI, not least because most philosophical debate centres less on the formal definition of AI—which is ultimately a technical matter -, and more on the extent to which AI can be regarded as analogous to, or distinct from, human intelligence.

Consider, for example, Searle's celebrated "Chinese Room" thought experiment (1980), which rejects the very possibility of Strong AI (see Sect. 2.1.1). This subject has animated and still animates philosophical debate: it engages not only the long-standing dispute between proponents of strong, or general, AI (Domingos, 2015) and those favouring weak, or narrow, AI, but also broader inquiries into where the line should be drawn between mechanical processing and conscious experience.

Questions that can be asked of students, adapted to their age, to promote discussion might include:

- Is a rock intelligent? Why?
- Is a sunflower intelligent?
- Is a dog intelligent?
- Is an octopus intelligent?
- Is a dog or an octopus more intelligent?

To introduce the concept of artificial emulations of human capabilities, questions such as:

- Is a calculator intelligent?
- Is a mobile phone intelligent?
- Is a computer intelligent?

Finally, reflections can be stimulated on the differences between humans and machines and in what field one can be considered better than the other through stimuli such as:

- **Computers/robots** are faster in calculations, do not make mistakes, do not get bored, remember better, do not get tired, do not need rest, etc.
- **Humans**: have emotions, creativity, affections, can enjoy the pleasure of food, rest, reading, etc.

2.2 *Teaching Computational Thinking: Papert's Turtle and Unplugged Coding*

When Turing posed the question "*Can machines think*?" he pointed out the extreme difficulty of making sense of this question and also, to some extent, its absurdity. Following Floridi (2023) it is therefore more appropriate to speak of *digital agency*, implying that what is generated by a machine is not the result of intelligence, as discussed in the previous section, but rather of intelligent acting—that is, a series of actions that, in line with Turing's original thought, emulate human intelligence.

As explained in Sect. 2.1.1, computers operate on only two symbols that allow them to perform both arithmetic and logical operations—that is, without going into technical details, they are able to make choices based on the value (TRUE/FALSE) of a bit:

IF [a given condition is TRUE].

THEN [perform action A]
ELSE [perform action B]

This sequence, however mechanical, can provide very interesting results and insights. Consider, for example, a simple game in which there are eleven matches on a table and two players who take turns collecting one, two, or three. The one who forces the opponent to collect the last match wins.

If we play for the first time with another human being, let us imagine remotely via a computer screen, the outcomes will probably be roughly evenly distributed between us and our opponent. Suppose, however, we provide our opponent (let's call them A, who gets the first move, while we will naturally be B) with the following instructions:

1. Collect two matches
2. Have B play
3. IF [the matches are finished] THEN [you won!!!] ELSE [go to instruction "4"]
4. IF [B picked up 1 match] THEN [execute instruction "5"] ELSE [go to instruction "6"]
5. Collect 2 matches then go to instruction "2"
6. IF [B collected 2 matches] THEN [go to instruction "7"] ELSE [go to instruction "8"]
7. Collect 2 matches then go to instruction "2"
8. Pick up 1 match then go to instruction "2"

With this sequence of operations our opponent will always win, at least when he/she moves first. We might imagine that, after a while, our opponent grows bored and lets the machine carry on, a machine that, under these conditions, would always win. In this case, from our side of the screen, we would be unable to tell whether we were playing against a human or a computer.

Although a machine that merely executes a fixed set of instructions might seem quite unintelligent to an outside observer, it could strike us—unaware of the underlying procedure—as a remarkably capable and gifted opponent. However, this example, simple as it is, outlines some fundamental aspects that underlie the artificial intelligence debate.

The first point concerns imitation. Although the machine cannot be called intelligent in the sense outlined in Sect. 2.2.1, within the limits of this example it can be said to display intelligent acting, because its play resembles that of a human applying intelligence to the game.

The second element highlights how some outward features of intelligent acting can be achieved by algorithmic means—that is, by a mechanical procedure such that it is possible to obtain the result by the simple execution of a set of instructions without the performer necessarily knowing the problem and its nature (Berlinski, 2000). Of course, if the execution of the procedure is mechanical, the formulation of the procedure (i.e., the algorithm) clearly is not and requires the definition of steps that are often instinctive and/or difficult for humans to formalise (Cormen et al., 2022).

In this border zone between intelligence, intelligent acting, logical-deductive thinking, and mechanical procedure lies computational thinking. The concept of computational thinking was first expressed by Papert and was formalised by computer scientist Wing, who defined it as "the thought processes involved in formulating problems and their solutions so that the solutions are represented in a form that can be effectively carried out by an information-processing agent" (Cuny et al., 2010).

Computational thinking is the basis of coding, the language with which humans communicate with machines, but it actually has a wider scope, being a strategy for solving more or less complex situations. Teaching computational thinking within a gamification context, especially for younger students, can be leveraged to help them understand how a machine "thinks"—or better, as Floridi (2023) suggests, acts—and, at the same time, which limits a machine may encounter when executing an algorithm, and what kind of intelligence is required to overcome them (Weng et al., 2024).

Indeed, when a machine processes vast and often heterogeneous datasets, the limitations of conventional computational procedures become evident (see Sect. 1.1 in chapter "The Operational Dimension: Uses and Applications"). In the real world, data carry a high degree of ambiguity—consider, for instance, the difference between handwritten and printed text—so a different approach from the one outlined above is required. Consider a simple request: sort a 52-card deck first by suit—hearts, diamonds, clubs, spades—and, within each suit, from ace to king.

A classic algorithm, bubble sort, repeatedly compares adjacent cards and swaps them until the deck is ordered. This method is straightforward, though far from efficient. By contrast, most humans would spread the cards on a table, visually cluster them into suits, and then refine each group—an approach guided by pattern recognition rather than rigid instruction following.

The first technique exemplifies a mechanical algorithm embedded in a computer program; the second resembles the behaviour of many AI and, specifically, machine—learning systems, which—as noted in Sect. 2.1.1—autonomously infer patterns (see also Sect. 1.2 in chapter "The Critical Dimension: Understanding and Evaluation Beyond Automation").

Two points are worth stressing. First, an algorithm such as bubble sort can exist as a *pure abstraction*, independent of any specific dataset, while AI cannot dispense with data since it learns and refines its outputs precisely through data. For this reason, the concept of data is fundamental and will be examined in depth in later chapters. Second, because AI is ultimately implemented on computers, it still relies on sets of instructions executed by the machine. Computational thinking, therefore, has by no means lost its pedagogical relevance; on the contrary, it remains essential for understanding the dialogue between human and machine.

How, then, can we engage children and adolescents in computational thinking and harness its educational values? One fruitful path is to draw on the work of Papert, who, in addition to being a distinguished mathematician and computer scientist, is widely regarded as a seminal educational theorist who in 1967 developed LOGO (Solomon et al., 2020) as a language that would enable children to "converse" with computers. In fact, LOGO is an educational programming language, suitable for beginners, particularly for children, whom Papert (1993, p. 9) considered to be animated by a "passionate and enduring love affair with the computer."

LOGO achieved global popularity through Papert's Turtle (Papert, 2002), a visual programming environment where simple instruction sequences move an on-screen object around a geometric plane. LOGO's successor is Scratch, a graphically richer and more user-friendly application, although some authors argue that this visual simplification may lead to conceptual shortcomings (Formiconi, 2018).

From Papert's early work to the present day, an extensive body of literature has flourished around LOGO and its derivative applications (Papert and Solomon, 1971, Harvey, 1997; Resnick, 2017; Belessova et al., 2024; Batni et al., 2024), together with a wealth of online open educational resources. Although both platforms are very simple and suitable for learners of any age, they still require prior knowledge about and familiarity with computers that some children may not yet possess.

To bridge this gap, we suggest a preliminary computer-free activity that can be implemented without the use of a machine, and which is commonly referred to as *unplugged coding* (Chen et al., 2023). It involves drawing a path, even an obstacle course, on a board or on the classroom floor, and asking children to reach the goal using only three moves: "GO FORWARD," "TURN RIGHT," and "TURN LEFT."

Once the children have written the moves they believe will succeed (for example, on separate cards), the instructions are handed to a classmate who plays the role of the robot and must execute them exactly as given. In the event that an instruction is wrong and leads the robot into a dead end, or the teacher interposes an obstacle that was not initially foreseen, a discussion can be triggered about how a machine is constrained by incorrect instructions and additional "intelligence" might be needed to overcome such hurdles. In this scenario, the introduction of a new command, "TURN BACK," may be necessary to help the robot escape the unexpected dead-end situation, thereby demonstrating that the instruction set must expand as task complexity increases.

References

AI HLEG - High-level expert group on artificial intelligence (2019), Ethics Guidelines for Trustworthy AI, European Commission, Brussels.

Ameen, L. T., Yousif, M. R., Alnoori, N. A. J., & Majeed, B. H. (2024). The impact of artificial intelligence on computational thinking in education at university. *International Journal of Engineering Pedagogy (iJEP), 14*(5), 192–203. https://doi.org/10.3991/ijep.v14i5.49995

Amirova A. *et al.* (2021), *10 Years of Human-NAO Interaction Research: A Scoping Review*, in Frontiers in Robotics and AI, 8, 744526.

Batni, B., Junaini, S. N., Sidi, J., Mustafa, W. A., & Awang Ismail, Z. I. (2024). Current research trends of Scratch block based programming for K-12: A systematic review. Journal of Advanced Research in Applied Sciences and Engineering Technology, 51(2), 138–152. https://doi.org/10.37934/araset.51.2.138152

Belessova, D., Ibashova, A., Zhidebayeva, A., Shaimerdenova, G., & Nakhipova, V. (2024). The impact of "Scratch" on student engagement and academic performance in primary schools. Open Education Studies, 6(1), Article 20220228. https://doi.org/10.1515/edu-2022-0228

Berlinski, D. (2000). The advent of the algorithm: The 300 year journey from an idea to the computer. Harcourt, Boston.

Blum-Ross A. *et al.* (2018), *Looking forward: Technological and social change in the lives of European children and young people. Report for the ICT coalition for children online*, ICT Coalition, Brussels.

Boden, M. A. (2016). *AI: Its Nature and Future*. Oxford University Press, Oxford.

Bolshaw, P., & Josephidou, Jo (2023). Understanding the Media in Young Children's Lives. An Introduction to the Key Debates. Routledge, Abington.

Buckingham D. (2013), *The Material Child: Growing Up in Consumer Culture, Polity Press, Cambridge.*

Burns T., Gottschalk F. (eds.) (2020), *Education in the Digital Age: Healthy and Happy Children*, *Educational Research and Innovation*, OECD Publishing, Paris.

Charisi, V. *et al.* (2022), *Artificial Intelligence and the Rights of the Child: Towards an Integrated Agenda for Research and Policy*, EUR 31048 EN, Publications Office of the European Union, Luxembourg.

Chen P. *et al.* (2023), *Fostering computational thinking through unplugged activities: A systematic literature review and meta-analysis*, in International Journal of STEM Education, 10, pp. 1–25.

Cormen T. H. *et al.* (2022), *Introduction to Algorithms*, MIT University Press, Cambridge, MA.

Cuny J., Snyder L., Wing J.M. (2010), *Demystifying Computational Thinking for Non-Computer Scientists*, work in progress (https://www.cs.cmu.edu/~CompThink/resources/TheLinkWing.pdf).

Dick, Philip K. (1968). *Do Androids Dream of Electric Sheep?* Doubleday & Company, New York,

Domingos P. (2015). *The Master Algorithm: How the Quest for the Ultimate Learning Machine Will Remake Our World*. Basic Books, New York.

Feigenbaum E.A., Feldman J. (1963), *Computers and thought*, McGraw-Hill, New York, NY.

Floridi L. (2014), *The Fourth Revolution: How the Infosphere is Reshaping Human Reality*, Oxford University Press, Oxford.

Floridi L. (2015), *The Onlife Manifesto. Being Human in a Hyperconnected Era*, Springer London.

Floridi L. (2023). *The Ethics of Artificial Intelligence: Principles, Challenges, and Opportunities* (Illustrated ed.). Oxford University Press, Oxford.

Formiconi A.R. (2018). *A step back into the future: text-based coding to foster creative thinking skills at school*, in M. K. Borges, M. Ranieri, L. Menichetti (eds.), Teacher Education & Training on ICT between Europe and Latin America, Aracne, Roma, pp. 153–64.

Frau-Meigs, D., Kotilainen, S., Pathak-Shelat, M., Hoechsmann, M., & R. Poyntz, S. (eds.) (2021). *The Handbook of Media Education Research*. John Wiley & Sons, Inc. https://doi.org/10.1002/9781119166900

Gardner H. (1983), *Frames of Mind: The Theory of Multiple Intelligences*, Basic, New York, NY.

Gardner H. (2009), *Birth and the spreading of a "meme,"* in [Chen J. Q., Moran S, Gardner H]. (eds.). *Multiple intelligences around the world*, Jossey-Bass, San Francisco, CA, pp. 3–16.

Goodfellow I. *et al.* (2014), *Generative Adversarial Nets* in Advances in Neural Information Processing Systems, 27, pp. 1–9.

Gurney K. (1997), *An introduction to neural networks*, UCL Press, London.

Halder, S., & Saha, S. (2023). *The Routledge Handbook of Education Technology*. Routledge, Abington.

Harvey, B. K. (1997). *Computer Science Logo Style (Vols. 1–3)*. Cambridge, MA: MIT Press.

Hobbs, R. (2021). *Media Literacy in Action: Questioning the Media*. Rowman & Littlefield Publishers New York.

International Telecommunication Union. (2024). *Measuring digital development: Facts and figures 2024*. International Telecommunication Union.

Knox, J. (2019). *What does the 'post digital' mean for education? Three critical perspectives on the digital, with implications for educational research and practice*. Postdigital Science and Education, 1(2), 357–370. https://doi.org/10.1007/s42438-019-00045-y

Landers, M. S. (2025). *Modern Prometheus: tracing the ill-defined path to AGI*. AI & Society, 1–19. https://doi.org/10.1007/s00146-025-02363-1

LeCun Y., Bengio Y., Hinton, G. (2015), *Deep learning*, in "Nature," 521(7553), 436–44.

Lipman, M. (1976), *Philosophy for children*, in "Metaphilosophy," 7(1), pp. 17–39.

Livingstone S., Bovill M. (Eds.) (2013), *Children and their changing media environment: A European comparative study*. Routledge, London.

Mascheroni, G., & Siibak, A. (2021). *Datafied Childhoods. Data Practices and Imaginaries in Children's Lives*. Peter Lang, New York.

Mayor A. (2018), *Gods and Robots: Myths, Machines, and Ancient Dreams of Technology*, Princeton University Press, Princeton, NJ, (1st ed.).

McCulloch W.S., Pitts W. (1943), *A logical calculus of the ideas immanent in nervous activity*, in "Bulletin of Mathematical Biophysics," 5, pp. 115–33.

M. Minsky, and S. Papert (1968) *Perceptrons. An Introduction to Computational Geometry*. MIT Press, Cambridge.

Mitchell M. (2020), *Artificial intelligence. A guide for thinking human beings*, First Picador paperback edition. Picador, London.

OECD (2025), How's Life for Children in the Digital Age?, OECD Publishing, Paris. https://doi.org/10.1787/0854b900-en

Page Jeffery, C. (2025). *Parenting in a Digital World. Beyond Media Panics Towards a New Theory of Parental Mediation*. Routledge, Abingdon on Thames, UK.

Papert S. (1980), *Mindstorms: Children, computers, and powerful ideas*, Basic Books, Inc, New York, NY.

Papert, S. (1993). *The children's machine: rethinking school in the age of the computer*. BasicBooks, New York.

Papert S. (2002), *The Turtle's Long Slow Trip: Macro-Educological Perspectives on Microworlds*, in "Journal of Educational Computing Research," 27(1), pp. 7–27.

Papert, S., & Solomon, C. (1971). *Twenty Things to Do with a Computer* (Artificial Intelligence Memo No. 248). Massachusetts Institute of Technology, Artificial Intelligence Laboratory, Cambridge.

Postman, N. (1982). *The disappearance of childhood*. Delacorte Press. Chicago

Ranieri, M. (2019). *Teaching with Media*. In: Renee Hobbs and Paul Mihailidis (Editors-in-Chief), Gianna Cappello, Maria Ranieri, and Benjamin Thevenin (Associate Editors). The International Encyclopedia of Media Literacy, pp. 1–11, Hoboken, NJ: JohnWiley & Sons, Inc. https://doi.org/10.1002/978 1118978238.ieml0233

Raugh, M., & Probst, S. (2019). *The Leibniz catenary and approximation of e: An analysis of his unpublished calculations*. Historia Mathematica, 49, 1–19. https://doi.org/10.1016/j.hm.2019.06.001

Resnick, M. (2017). *Lifelong Kindergarten: Cultivating Creativity through Projects, Passion, Peers, and Play* (Illustrated ed.). Cambridge, MA: MIT Press. https://doi.org/10.7551/mitpress/11017.001.0001

Searle J. (1980), *Minds, Brains and Programs. Behavioral and Brain Sciences*, 3(3), Cambridge University Press, Cambridge, pp. *417–24*

Solomon C. *et al.* (2020), *History of Logo*. Proc. ACM Program. Lang., Vol. 4, No. HOPL, Article 79.

Standage T. (2002), *The Turk. The life and times of the famous eighteenth-century chess-playing automaton*, Walker & Company, New York

Sternberg R.J. (2000), *Handbook of Intelligence*, Cambridge University Press, Cambridge.

Swade, D. (2000). *The Cogwheel Brain: Charles Babbage and the Quest to Build the First Computer*. London, Little, Brown and Company.

Swade D. (2022), *The History of Computing: A Very Short Introduction*, Oxford University Press, Oxford.

Tisseron S. (2013), *3-6-9-12 Apprivoiser les écrans et grandir*, Eres, Toulouse.

Turing A.M. (1950), *Computing machinery and intelligence*, in "Mind," 59, pp. 433–60.

UNICEF (2021), *Policy guidance on AI for children*. (https://www.unicef.org/globalinsight/media/2356/file/UNICEF-Global-Insight-policy-guidance-AI-children-2.0-2021.pdf).

Warwick, K. (2012). *Artificial Intelligence: The Basics* (1st ed.). Routledge. https://doi.org/10.4324/9780203802878

Weng, X., Ye, H., Dai, Y., & Ng, O. L. (2024). *Integrating Artificial Intelligence and Computational Thinking in Educational Contexts: A Systematic Review of Instructional Design and Student Learning Outcomes. Journal of Educational Computing Research*, *62*(6), 1420–1450. https://doi.org/10.1177/07356331241248686

The Operational Dimension: Uses and Applications

Abstract This chapter examines the operational dimension of AI Literacy, focusing on how modern AI systems learn from data and are applied in various contexts. It begins by contextualising the historical shift from the symbolic, instruction-based paradigm (GOFAI) to the now-dominant subsymbolic, data-driven approach of machine learning (ML). The core mechanisms of ML are explained, detailing its main types: supervised, unsupervised, and reinforcement learning. This chapter then provides an in-depth analysis of the current state-of-the-art, explaining the Transformer architecture that powers Large Language Models (LLMs) and Generative AI. Following this technical exposition, a typology of AI applications is presented, categorised by user profiles (programmers, professionals, citizens) and with a specific focus on their use in education. To translate these complex concepts into practice, this chapter concludes by proposing two pedagogical methods: using the trial-and-error technique to teach the principles of classification and employing gamification to help learners understand the processes of estimation and prediction in AI.

Keywords Machine Learning (ML) · Large Language Models (LLMs) · Data-driven approach · Classification · Estimation and prediction

M. Ranieri et al., *Artificial Intelligence in Schools*, Digital Education and Learning, https://doi.org/10.1007/978-3-032-15919-9_3

1 Themes and Issues

1.1 From Instructions to Data: Towards Machine Learning

The history of Artificial Intelligence (AI), as outlined in the previous chapter, has alternated periods of enthusiasm with prolonged "AI winters," and has been traversed by vigorous discussions that have shaped the field over the years. One of the most influential debates was the dispute between supporters of the symbolic approach (known as "Good Old-Fashioned Artificial Intelligence" or GOFAI) and advocates of the subsymbolic tradition (or neural networks), which took place towards the end of the 1960s (Boden, 2016). Proponents of the symbolic approach, including researchers such as Papert and Minsky, conceptualised AI through the lens of logic and symbolic representation, based on explicit knowledge codification, employing symbols and rules. The latter, which are often created by domain experts, are used to deduce new information through logical procedures, organised through modules or discrete units, facilitating thought specialisation. One of the main strengths of this approach is its transparency: the clarity with which knowledge is represented makes these systems easily interpretable (Russell and Norvig, 2009). By contrast, researchers in the subsymbolic camp—among them Rosenblatt, Rumelhart, Hinton, Williams—, in sustaining neural networks drew inspiration from psychology and biology, arguing that intelligence could emerge from low-level processes modelled on the brain and emphasised data-driven learning. Unlike the symbolic approach, where the machine must be explicitly programmed, a system based on neural networks "learns" by recognising data patterns and improving/adapting dynamically throughout experience. Information processing also occurs differently: if in symbolic AI information is processed sequentially, neural networks process information in parallel, mirroring the functioning of biological neurons (McClelland et al., 1986; McCulloch and Pitts, 1943).

Turning to one of the most contested issues, Minsky and Papert's (1969) monograph *Perceptrons* is particularly meaningful. In this volume, the researchers examined the properties and limits of the perceptron, that is, the single-layer neural network model introduced by Rosenblatt (1962) and demonstrated that such simple neural models were intrinsically limited in their computational capacity and were also unable to solve certain types of fundamental logical functions, notably XOR. In other words, although perceptrons offered a new approach to learning and model adaptation, they were not the *panacea* for all computational challenges. This work undermined the confidence that neural networks had earned until then, giving rise to one of the numerous *querelles* on AI (Boden, 2016). Minsky and Papert then further contrasted these limitations with the versatility of symbolic AI: rule-based systems, they argued, could tackle a breadth and depth of problem-solving tasks that perceptrons, in their existing form, could not match.

These two approaches, symbolic and subsymbolic, have generated years of debates and comparisons. Although in this chapter we will focus on the subsymbolic tradition—for reasons that will soon become clear—it would not be correct to consider one of the approaches as less important or outdated. Over time, in fact, the community of scholars has recognised that both approaches have their merits and can be complementary (Boden, 2016). Hybrid approaches, which combine symbolic representation with deep learning (DL), based on subsymbolic elements, are emerging as particularly promising solutions to address the challenges of AI in its most recent developments.

The concomitance of several factors such as the increase in computational power enabling the development of more complex neural networks, the growing availability of data, the renewed attention and consequent funding from major stakeholders, and the limitations shown by the explicit instruction approach when dealing with complex tasks delegated to AI (see more later), has led, since the 2000s, to what has been called as the "resurrection" of neural networks (Boden, 2016, p. 116).

As mentioned in Sect. 2.2 in chapter "The Cognitive Dimension: Historical Background and Key Concepts", when confronted with vast and articulated datasets, such as unstructured text, complex images to classify, or real-time data streams, sequential and algorithmic processing, typical of the computational approach, can become inefficient and limiting in the face of data's complexity and uncertainty. The obstacles this perspective encounters when handling large volumes of data are manifold (Russell and Norvig, 2009). First, such processing demands considerable time and computational resources: analysing a massive dataset may, in fact, require an enormous number of calculations that sequential execution alone cannot sustain. Second, the computational approach struggles with difficulties in addressing the unstructured nature of complex data. In fact, effective analysis of such datasets presupposes a broadening of the study field, so as to also embrace the understanding of context, semantic relationships and linguistic nuances, in the case of dealing with, for example, textual processing. Finally, the set of instructions provided with this approach might not be able to resolve aspects of uncertainty and variability. Real data often contains noise, fluctuations, and ambiguity that call for more sophisticated, adaptive techniques. In these situations, the classical computational approach risks proving not sufficiently adaptable and flexible, thereby limiting its ability to model and interpret grey areas (Allen et al., 2023).

All this suggests that, to build AI systems capable of interacting effectively with the real world, solving novel problems, and continuously improving their performance, we need a different perspective: a data-driven approach that enables AI systems to "learn" from unstructured and semi-structured data, and to adapt dynamically to previously unseen situations.

In recent years, data have therefore assumed an increasingly central role in production and exchange activities, to the point of being regarded as an economic asset in their own right. Thanks to advances in information and communication technologies, organisations now collect data of every kind, process them in real time to support decision-making, and store them permanently for future reuse or to extract new knowledge. According to IDC's latest Global DataSphere forecast (2024–2028) projects that the volume of data created, captured, and replicated worldwide will reach about 394 ZB by 2028 (>24% from 2023), whereas earlier IDC forecasts (2021–2025) estimated around 181 ZB by 2025—up from roughly 33 ZB in 2018, underscoring the unprecedented scale of datafication that is reshaping economies and societies (Wright, 2024).

Of course, data considered in isolation are of limited significance; they acquire value only when organised. This makes the processing phase central to the data value chain, transforming raw data into interpretable and actionable information. For such analysis, organisations increasingly rely on algorithms—especially learning algorithms—that exploit advanced AI techniques such as machine learning (ML) to extract new knowledge.

With these algorithms, the resulting models are inherently volatile, which means that they change over time. This volatility arises partly because the reference conditions, notably the underlying data, continuously evolve and partly because the models are iteratively refined to improve accuracy. It also grants them a degree of behavioural freedom, enabling machines to analyse vast amounts of data autonomously and to discover hidden patterns and correlations.

Alongside quantity, data quality as well plays a decisive role in AI, especially when data volume is limited. In these cases, accurate, complete, and representative samples are indispensable for models to learn effectively and yield reliable results. Data quality depends on several factors, including data sources, collection procedures, annotation, and cleaning. Rigorous methodologies and practices are therefore essential to ensure that the data are trustworthy, error-free, and faithful to the real-world phenomena being modelled; otherwise, bias can propagate (for a definition of bias and further information, see §3.1.3).

Because AI data are dynamic rather than static, models must be updated continuously to stay aligned with the real world. Data management and updating are thus integral to the AI life cycle, allowing intelligent systems to remain adaptable and aligned as their operating contexts evolve. This data-driven philosophy underpins two major AI subfields: ML and DL, both of which rely on extensive data to teach systems how to perform tasks, though in markedly different ways (Russell and Norvig, 2009).

ML is an AI branch resting on the idea that systems can learn from data, identify patterns, and make decisions with minimal human intervention. This field of study is situated at the intersection of computer science, statistics, and data engineering, and represents the driving force of many current technological innovations, from personalised recommendation systems to autonomous vehicles. In essence, the expression *machine learning* denotes a system's capacity to improve its own performance over time. As noted in §1.1 in chapter "The Cognitive Dimension: Historical Background and Key Concepts", system learning, similarly to human learning, arises through experience. Specifically, ML systems "learn" from enormous amounts of data: by ingesting them, the model identifies patterns, internalises them, and then makes predictions or decisions without explicit programming.

ML can be divided into three principal branches: supervised learning, unsupervised learning and reinforcement learning, each grounded in distinct principles and methodologies (Russell and Norvig, 2009). Let us examine them in detail.

Supervised learning (SL) is the most widely adopted branch of ML. In this case, the model is trained on a dataset of labelled examples, meaning that for each input we already know the desired output. The aim is for the model to learn the relationship between inputs (features) and output (label), and subsequently generalise that knowledge to previously unseen, unlabelled data. Typical supervised-learning tasks include: (i) *classification*, where each observation is assigned to a discrete category, and (ii) *regression*, where the goal is to predict a continuous value. An example of supervised ML could be a model trained on a large dataset of animal images labelled by their respective species. In this case, the model would use this information to learn to recognise the distinctive characteristics of each species and could then apply this knowledge to classify new animal images with a high degree of accuracy (Bishop, 2006).

In the case of unsupervised learning (UL), instead, the model operates on unlabelled data and has to identify latent structures or patterns within them. Two canonical tasks are: (1) clustering, which groups similar observations together, and (2) dimensionality reduction, which compresses data into a lower-dimensional representation while preserving salient information. A typical example is customer segmentation in marketing, where customers are grouped into distinct segments based on patterns that emerge from their purchasing behaviour.

Finally, reinforcement learning (RL) is a branch of ML in which an agent learns to make decisions by interacting with the environment aiming at maximising a cumulative notion of reward. More specifically, the agent takes actions in an environment to achieve a goal. For each action, the agent receives feedback from the environment, which can be positive (a reward), if the action brings it closer to the goal, or negative (a punishment), if the action moves it away. The agent learns a strategy or policy, that is, a mapping from states to actions, that maximises the sum of future rewards. RL is guided by (1) exploration and (2) exploitation. In the exploration phase, the agent takes random actions to discover unknown information about the environment. In the exploitation phase, the agent uses the information learned to make the decision that seems to be the best. A fundamental aspect of RL is finding a balance between exploring new actions and exploiting those already known to be effective. A classic example is training a computer to play chess. The computer (the agent) makes a decision (a move), receives a response from the environment (the opponent's move), and obtains a reward (winning, losing, or drawing the game). The computer's goal is to learn a strategy that maximises its chances of winning.

As previously noted, a prominent subfield of machine learning is deep learning (DL), which is also grounded in artificial neural networks. These networks can learn and improve their performance via backpropagation, a procedure that adjusts the weights of neural connections on the basis of the error between the output predicted by the model and the true target; they comprise multiple layers of interconnected nodes—or *neurons*—, each of which can process information and pass the result to the nodes of the next layer (Jordan and Mitchell, 2015).

Neural networks with many layers (hence the adjective "deep") can capture complex patterns in data, but demands not only sophisticated mathematical models, but also large dataset, and substantial computational resources (Russell and Norvig, 2009). As mentioned in §1.1 in chapter "The Cognitive Dimension: Historical Background and Key Concepts", whereas conventional ML models typically require manual feature engineering to highlight relevant aspects of the data, DL models can automatically identify the features needed to achieve the desired performance. This capability has enabled DL to attain impressive results in a wide range of applications, from image generation to speech recognition, from automatic translation to autonomous driving. Finally, with regard to the most recent developments, as highlighted in chapter "The Cognitive Dimension: Historical Background and Key Concepts", since 2014 we have witnessed the rise of Generative Artificial Intelligence (GAI) (Goodfellow et al., 2014).

1.2 The Era of Generative Artificial Intelligence and Large Language Models

Building on the historical foundations traced in the previous sections, from mechanical automata to machine learning, the field of artificial intelligence has entered what many regard as its most transformative phase: the era of generative artificial intelligence (GAI).

The conceptual trajectory that led to today's generative models began with early distributional language models and, a little later, with deep generative architectures such as variational auto-encoders (VAEs). A decisive breakthrough came in 2014, when Generative Adversarial Networks (GANs) reframed generation as a creative contest between a *generator* and a *discriminator*, enabling the production of strikingly realistic synthetic images (Goodfellow et al., 2014). Yet GANs still struggled with language. The turning point for text arrived three years later with the Transformer architecture introduced in the seminal paper "*Attention is all you need*" (Vaswani et al., 2017).

To appreciate the significance of this development, it is helpful to contrast it briefly with previous AI paradigms. Traditional AI systems, including the symbolic AI discussed earlier, primarily relied on explicit rules and logical manipulations; classic expert systems, for instance, executed pre-programmed sequences of deductions. Even connectionist approaches such as earlier neural networks inspired by the brain's structure, while powerful at pattern recognition, were still limited in their ability to cope with the full complexity and ambiguity of unstructured data (e.g., natural language) or to generate entirely novel, coherent, and contextually relevant content at scale.

Generative AI, by contrast, encompasses models that extract underlying patterns and statistical regularities from vast datasets and then leverage this learned knowledge to synthesise new, original artefacts—be it text, images, audio, or code—that resemble, yet are distinct from, their training data.

The innovation that unlocked much of today's generative capabilities was the development of the transformer architecture. Introduced by Vaswani et al. (2017) at Google (Vaswani et al., 2017), the transformer model represented a radical shift from previous sequential processing methods, such as Recurrent Neural Networks (RNNs) and Long Short-Term Memory (LSTM) networks. These earlier architectures processed words in a sentence one by one, creating bottlenecks in capturing long-range dependencies (how words far apart in a text relate to each other) and limiting the ability to parallelise the training process on large datasets.

The transformer, by contrast, introduced the concept of self-attention mechanisms. In simplified terms, "attention" allows the model to weigh the importance of different parts of the input data when processing any given element. In the case of language, this means the model can simultaneously consider the relationships between all words in a text, regardless of their position. For instance, when attempting to determine the meaning of the word "bank" in a sentence, a self-attention mechanism can examine surrounding context—such as "river" and "flow," or "money" and "account"—to infer the appropriate meaning.

This is achieved by computing "attention scores" between the individual words (or *tokens*) in the input, effectively allowing the model to focus on the most relevant pieces of information at each step of its processing. Transformers perform this operation across multiple layers and through multiple "attention heads," enabling them to capture a rich complex web of syntactic and semantic relationships within the data. This capacity for massive parallel processing, coupled with their superior handling of context, was crucial in making it possible to train models far larger and more powerful than had previously been feasible.

Building directly on this architectural breakthrough, the era of Large Language Models (LLMs) was inaugurated. LLMs are, at their core, transformer models that have been scaled to immense proportions, both in the number of parameters they contain (values learned during training that often number in the tens or hundreds of billions, and occasionally even trillions) and in the vast volume of data on which they are trained. Such training corpora typically consist of enormous swathes of text and code scraped from the internet, digitised books, and a variety of other sources.

Prominent examples that have captured public and academic attention include OpenAI's GPT (Generative Pre-trained Transformer) series (e.g., Radford et al., 2018, 2019; Brown et al., 2020), Google's BERT (Bidirectional Encoder Representations from Transformers) (Devlin et al., 2019), PaLM (Pathways Language Model) (Chowdhery et al., 2023), and LaMDA; Meta's LLaMA (Large Language Model Meta AI) (Touvron et al., 2023); and many others.

A defining characteristic of these LLMs is the emergence of remarkable capabilities that often arise unexpectedly from this immense scale. Researchers have observed that, as models grow larger and are trained on more diverse data, they begin to exhibit abilities that were not explicitly programmed into them. These emergent capabilities can include performing few-shot or zero-shot learning (accomplishing tasks with very few or no examples), translating between languages they were never specifically instructed, solving mathematical-reasoning problems, writing different kinds of creative content, generating computer code, and engaging in surprisingly coherent and context-aware dialogues.

The training process for many state-of-the-art LLMs typically involves a two-stage approach. First is pre-training, during which the model learns to predict the next word (or a masked word) in a sequence by processing its enormous, unlabelled text corpus. This self-supervised process, though computationally intensive, allows the model to internalise intricate patterns of language, factual knowledge embedded in the text, and even some rudimentary forms of reasoning.

Following pre-training, many models undergo a fine-tuning stage. This can involve additional training on more specific datasets for particular tasks, or, increasingly, alignment techniques like Reinforcement Learning from Human Feedback (RLHF) (Ouyang et al., 2022). In RLHF, human trainers rank different model outputs, and this feedback is used to train a reward model, which then guides the LLM to produce outputs that are more helpful, harmless, and aligned with human preferences and conversational norms.

It is important to distinguish this generative capacity from earlier AI achievements. Whereas an AI system might once have been able only to classify an image as a cat or a dog, a generative model like OpenAI's DALL-E (Ramesh et al., 2021) or Stable Diffusion can create a new image of a cat or dog based on a textual description. Similarly, where an older system might merely parse a sentence, an LLM can write an entire essay. This ability to synthesise novel content that exhibits coherence, and often surprising originality, is a hallmark of the current generative wave.

The mechanisms underlying LLMs offer fascinating, though still actively researched, insights into how artificial systems can approximate aspects of complex information processing. Unlike traditional software that operates on explicit, predefined logic, LLMs function through what can be described as highly sophisticated pattern matching. They don't "understand" language or concepts in the human sense, which entails embodied experience, consciousness, and a deep causal model of the world. Instead, they are extraordinarily adept at predicting plausible sequences of tokens (words or sub-words) based on the statistical patterns internalised from their training data. When these predictions are chained together, the resulting text can appear remarkably thoughtful, contextually aware, and even creative.

However, this appearance of capability comes with inherent limitations that are crucial for educators and learners to grasp as part of developing critical AI literacy. LLMs are prone to *hallucinations*—generating confident-sounding yet factually incorrect or nonsensical information (see Sect. 1.2 in chapter "The Critical Dimension: Understanding and Evaluation Beyond Automation"). They can also reproduce, and occasionally amplify, biases present in the vast corpora on which they are trained, corpora that often reflect societal stereotypes relating to gender, race, and other characteristics (Bender et al., 2021).

Furthermore, LLMs lack genuine grounding in real-world experience, possess only the common sense that can be statistically inferred from text, and have no intrinsic capacity to verify the accuracy or ethical implications of their outputs. As Bender et al. (2021) powerfully argue in their work on the risks posed by "stochastic parrots," it is essential to understand an LLM as a system that manipulates linguistic form on the basis of probabilistic training, rather than one that truly comprehends meaning.

This emergence of powerful, widely accessible generative AI tools represents a paradigmatic shift not only in technological capability but also in the ways humans interact with information and create content. For the first time, individuals at large have access to artificial systems that can engage in complex dialogue, assist in drafting documents, generate creative works, and synthesise knowledge across a vast range of topics.

This development carries profound implications for education, particularly for the cognitive dimension of AI literacy. It compels us to rethink what it means to *know* something, how information is produced and validated, and how notions of authorship and creativity are evolving.

As we shall explore in more detail, these tools offer both opportunities and significant challenges. Students can now employ AI as a brainstorming partner, research assistant, or language-practice tool—possibilities that are potentially transformative. But the ease with which convincing, yet possibly misleading or biased, content can be generated underscores the urgent need for pedagogical strategies that encourage critical evaluation, source verification, and an ethical awareness of AI's operations and outputs.

Understanding the technical foundations of generative AI—the role of data, the transformer architecture, the model-training process, and the technology's inherent limitations—is therefore no longer a niche concern reserved for computer scientists. It has become a foundational competency for any citizen, learner, or educator navigating an increasingly AI-mediated world. What this era demands are neither blind acceptance nor blanket rejection of these technologies, but rather a critically informed engagement equipped to harness their potential responsibly while mitigating their risks.

To ground these broad implications in a concrete example, consider the specialised domain of AI for education. Recent advances have prompted what several scholars describe as a *fourth generation* of Intelligent Tutoring Systems (ITS). First-generation tutors (1970s–1990s) were rule-based expert systems such as *SOPHIE* or *STEAMER*; second-generation systems (mid-1990s–2010s) adopted cognitive-modelling frameworks like ACT-R; third-generation solutions (2010s–2021) combined learning analytics with large-scale adaptation engines (e.g.,

ALEKS). The current, fourth wave—often labelled LLM-driven ITS—employs large language models to support open-ended, conversational interaction while retaining the classical four-component architecture of *domain*, *student*, *tutoring*, and *interface* models (Nye, 2015; Maity & Deroy, 2024). Consequently, tools such as Khanmigo should be viewed not as a break with the ITS tradition, but as its latest evolutionary stage.

A second clarification concerns the widely cited typology of AI applications in higher education advanced by Zawacki-Richter et al. (2019). Although their review advanced Profiling & Prediction from Intelligent Tutoring Systems as separate analytic categories, the two functions are in practice inseparable: an ITS can adapt its pedagogy only insofar as it continually profiles the learner and predicts future performance on the basis of a student model (Pavlik et al., 2013). Throughout this chapter, therefore, we treat learner profiling as an enabling layer that underpins fourth generation ITS rather than as a mutually exclusive application class.

1.3 Main Types of AI Applications

AI is transforming our world in ways that few could have foreseen. From sophisticated machine learning algorithms that power search engines to the systems piloting autonomous-vehicle prototypes, artificial intelligence is now virtually omnipresent. Yet, despite its ubiquity, not all AI applications are created equal. Its manifestations can be grouped into distinct categories, each with its own peculiarities and challenges.

In this paragraph, we will explore the principal types of AI applications, organised according to their end user, whether they are AI application programmers, professionals who employ AI in their day-to-day work, or citizens who, often unconsciously, rely on AI in everyday life. This subdivision allows us to understand more clearly how AI is deployed in different contexts and for different purposes, and it helps us reflect on the scope and impact of the technology. In the second part of the paragraph, we examine in depth those applications that focus on the educational field.

AI applications for programmers: This category comprises the tools and platforms that are used to build and implement AI-based solutions. It encompasses open-source machine learning libraries and frameworks such as TensorFlow, Keras and PyTorch; full-stack data-processing and model-creation services such as Google Cloud AI, AWS SageMaker and Azure Machine Learning; and "AI-as-a-service" offerings that provide turnkey functionality, for instance **Google Cloud Vision** and **IBM Watson**. These tools are designed to simplify the development of AI-based solutions, enabling programmers to concentrate on problem-solving rather than on building learning algorithms from scratch. The chief requirements for using such applications are fluency in programming languages and a solid grasp of AI and ML concepts, whereas the main challenges include (a) keeping pace with rapid technological change and (b) ensuring transparency, robustness, and reliability. Developers must address issues such as managing bias in training data, the opacity of many ML models, and privacy risks arising from inappropriate data use.

AI applications for professionals: This category includes solutions that harness AI to boost the productivity and efficiency of professionals across sectors. Examples include data-analysis and visualisation suites that detect patterns and trends (e.g., Tableau, Oracle, Azure, Power BI); virtual assistants that manage calendars and automate routine processes (e.g., Siri, Google Assistant, Alexa); and software for image generation or retouching (e.g., Adobe Photoshop, Canva, Midjourney). Because their chief objective is to streamline workflows, these tools can radically reshape the way professionals perform their tasks, freeing time for more strategic and creative activities. Barriers to adoption include the need for baseline knowledge of AI mechanisms—skills that demand ongoing training—and the capacity to adapt such tools to one's specific work context, often in the face of resistance to change. Key risks arise from decisions based on predictions that may be erroneous or biased, the potential violation of customer privacy or loss of sensitive data, and the creeping de-responsibilisation of human judgement.

AI applications for citizens: This category encompasses all those AI-enabled applications that can be used directly by citizens in their daily lives and may involve a wide variety of tools and services. Intelligent voice assistants such as Siri, Alexa, and Google Assistant use AI to interpret voice commands and respond coherently. Personalised-recommendations engines on streaming platforms like Netflix and Spotify analyse user preferences and suggest content aligned with their tastes. Personal-health-monitoring apps can employ AI to interpret physiological data and propose customised exercise or diet plans. Intelligent navigation systems such as Waze and Google Maps rely on AI to process real-time traffic data and propose the fastest route. The overarching aim of these applications is to simplify and optimise daily life, providing tools that can assist users in multiple domains. The skills threshold required to operate such applications is generally kept to a minimum (cf. Sect. 1.2in chapter "The Cognitive Dimension: Historical Background and Key Concepts"), demanding only basic digital literacy. Nevertheless, ease of use does not eliminate risks related to privacy and security; it arises from uncontrolled data exploitation and from the opacity and limited interpretability of many AI systems.

As noted above, the deployment of these applications presents both opportunities and challenges that must be addressed to ensure effective and safe operation. Below, we recall several key issues, referring the reader to subsequent chapters for more detailed discussion.

A first critical issue concerns the biases present in data and how they are managed. Biases constitute a sort of distortion that can be introduced during data collection, selection or labelling, leading to a skewed or partial representation of reality and, consequently, to biased model outputs (Barocas et al., 2017; Perrotta, 2022). For instance, if the dataset used to train a facial-recognition model is unbalanced with respect to ethnicity or gender, the resulting system may behave discriminatorily. Mitigating data bias therefore requires a careful assessment of data quality and representativeness, complemented by strategies such as balanced-dataset curation and the application of debiasing techniques.

Another frequently cited concern involves privacy risks arising from the ever-growing volume of data—often sensitive and collected with varying degrees of transparency—employed by AI systems (UNESCO, 2021). Protecting privacy is crucial to ensure that personal and sensitive information is processed appropriately; this entails adherence to applicable data-protection laws and the implementation of robust security safeguards against unauthorised access. Users must be made aware of data-management practices, and their informed consent should be obtained for any use of personal data (AI HLEG, 2019).

As we shall see in chapter "The Critical Dimension: Understanding and Evaluation Beyond Automation", another source of potential opacity stems from the interpretability of AI models. Indeed, ML processes are frequently viewed as *black boxes*: they can yield highly accurate results, yet they cannot provide an equally clear account of the reasoning behind their decisions. This lack of transparency raises serious concerns about responsibility, ethics, and trust (Jobin et al., 2019). It is therefore essential to devise approaches and techniques that render AI models increasingly interpretable and accessible, enabling users to understand how specific choices are made and ensuring fairness in the use of data. Content security likewise remains a crucial consideration, because data are vulnerable to threats such as alteration, theft, or improper use (UNESCO, 2021). Consequently, strengthening security standards becomes imperative, and organisations must adopt rigorous data-management policies aimed at safeguarding the integrity and confidentiality of information.

Table 1 summarises the characteristics of the main types of AI applications, providing a description of their uses and associated risks.

Narrowing the focus to the educational field, we can identify tools aimed at personalising learning, improving student performance, and supporting teachers (Miao and Holmes, 2021; Yim and Su, 2025). UNESCO (2021) has provided a mapping of AI systems in education, distinguishing the following applications:

- **Intelligent tutoring systems**: students can benefit from tutoring systems that leverage AI to deliver personalised instruction tailored to their needs. These systems analyse student learning data—such as test scores and exercise responses—to identify areas of strength and weakness. In addition, they provide targeted feedback, study suggestions, and supplementary resources that help learners improve their skills effectively.
- **Continuous assessment of learning**: AI can support ongoing assessment during both online and in-person learning activities. By examining variables such as time spent on a task, interaction patterns, and progress achieved, algorithms can detect students who may be struggling or who require additional support. This capability enables teachers to intervene promptly and offer personalised assistance that addresses learners' individual needs.
- **Recommendations of educational content**: AI can generate customised recommendations for instructional materials. Drawing on data about learner performance, preferences, and assessment results, recommendation engines propose additional materials, resources and activities that match each student's interests and abilities, thereby fostering more engaging, stimulating, and needs-responsive learning.
- **Automated assessment**: AI can also streamline the evaluation process. By analysing responses to, for instance, multiple-choice questions, AI systems can score student work rapidly and consistently, saving teachers time and ensuring objective results. Moreover,

Table 1 Types of AI applications by profile: characteristics, objectives, challenges, and risks

	AI for Programmers	*AI for Professionals*	*AI for Citizens*
Definition	Tools that help programmers build, train, and implement AI models	Tools that help professionals improve their efficiency and productivity at work	Tools that employ AI to improve daily life and personalise user experience
Examples of applications	Cloud ML services (Google Cloud AI, Azure Machine Learning, Amazon SageMaker, IBM Watson), open-source deep learning libraries (TensorFlow, Keras)	Software for data visualisation (Tableau), business intelligence (Power BI), image generation or retouching (Adobe Photoshop, Midjourney)	Intelligent voice assistants (Siri, Alexa, and Google Assistant), personalised recommendations (Netflix, Spotify), health monitoring applications, intelligent navigation systems (Waze, Google Maps)
Objective	Simplify and facilitate the development of applications, even for developers who are not specialised in this field	Improve the effectiveness and efficiency of professionals in various sectors by providing tools that can automate or enhance different aspects of their work	Make routine daily activities simpler and more efficient by providing tools that can assist in various aspects of life
Required skills	Knowledge of programming languages, familiarity with AI and ML concepts, ability to manage and analyse large amounts of data	Basic knowledge of AI, including its benefits and limitations, and the ability to apply AI tools within the context of one's work	Ability to use digital technologies and awareness of data security and privacy issues

	AI for Programmers	*AI for Professionals*	*AI for Citizens*
Challenges	Keeping pace with rapid technology developments while ensuring transparency, robustness, and reliability	Implementation within existing sectors, resistance to change, and the need for continuous training	Data privacy and security, and a lack of awareness in understanding AI and its limitations
Risks	Bias in training data, lack of robustness and transparency in ML models, and privacy violations resulting from inappropriate use of data	Decisions made based on predictions that may be erroneous or compromised by bias, potential violations of customer privacy, and erosion of personal responsibility in decision-making	Risks related to privacy and security due to the uncontrolled use of data, as well as a lack of transparency and interpretability

AI can supply detailed feedback that helps learners understand their errors, refine their efforts, and enhance the overall quality of their learning experience.

- **Identification of student learning patterns**: AI can mine student learning data to uncover patterns and trends in study habits. Such insights help teachers grasp individual learning profiles and adapt instructional strategies accordingly. For example, if the system detects that a learner assimilates information more effectively through visual means, the teacher might provide tailored supports such as visual materials, interactive simulations, educational video games, or comic-based readings.

These examples represent only a fraction of the myriad applications of AI in education. Fundamentally, they illustrate the promise of truly personalised instruction, one that accounts for each student's unique characteristics, aptitudes, learning pace, and aspirations.

Tables 2 and 3 synthesises the different types of AI tools for education and provides examples of specific applications.

Similarly, focusing on GenAI applications, Table 3 offers a more granular view, organising AI tools according to their educational purpose and application domains. This taxonomy highlights the breadth of AI's potential contributions across the full spectrum of teaching and learning activities:

- Content creation: AI can assist educators in generating diverse instructional materials, including quizzes and tests, slide presentations, educational images, videos, infographics, and mind maps. These tools reduce preparation time while enabling teachers to produce visually engaging and pedagogically sound resources tailored to their curriculum and students' needs.
- Assessment and feedback: AI streamlines the evaluation process through automatic grading of essays and assignments, generation of personalised feedback, creation of assessment rubrics, plagiarism and AI-content detection, and continuous progress tracking. These capabilities allow teachers to provide timely, consistent, and detailed feedback while managing the administrative burden of assessment more efficiently.

Table 2 Types of AI tools and examples of applications

Category	*Description*	*Examples*
Intelligent Tutoring Systems	Tools for personalised feedback	Khan Academy (Khanmigo), Duolingo, Socratic by Google
Automatic Assessment Tools	Automatic assessment tools for student assignments	EssayGrader, CoGrader, Brisk Teaching
Inattention Detection Tools	Student behaviour analysis software	ClassDojo (Sidekick AI), GoGuardian Teacher, Securly Classroom, Brightspace Analytics, D2L Corporation platforms
Learning Path Personalisation Tools	Software that adapts content based on student needs	Alta by Wiley (formerly Knewton), Smart Sparrow (Pearson-owned), McGraw Hill ALEKS, Realizeit, Cerego
Educational Resource Suggestion Systems	Tools to enrich learning with additional resources	MagicSchool.ai, Curipod, Perplexity
Learning Analytics Tools	Predictive software about student success/failure	Google Classroom built-in, Khan Academy dashboard, Quizizz
Generative AI Tools for Educators	A new class of GAI tools designed to support teachers with planning, content creation, and administrative tasks	MagicSchool AI (educator tools), Google NotebookLM, Khan Academy GPT integration
AI Learning Software	Digital artefacts for teaching AI	Cognimates, AI for Oceans, Teachable Machine, Machine Learning for Kids, MixLab, ecraft2learn, Gan Dissect, Unplugged AI, PlushPal, Scratch, Google's Teachable Machine
AI Learning Hardware	Physical devices for teaching AI	LEGO Education SPIKE Prime, Sphero (indi/BOLT), Digital Dream Labs Cozmo 2.0, VEX GO, WhalesBot, Hengbot educational robots

Table 3 AI tools by educational purpose and applications

Category	*Subcategory*	*Description*	*Free/Accessible Tools*	*Best For*
Content creation	Quiz & Tests	Generate interactive assessments	Khanmigo (Khan Academy) QuizGecko Brisk Teaching Quizizz AI, Wooclap	Teachers K-12
	Presentations	Create slide decks with AI	Slidesgo AI Gamma Canva Education SlidesAI (Google add-on)	Teachers all levels
	Images	Generate educational images	Canva Magic Media Adobe Firefly Teachable Machine	Visual content creation
	Videos	Create educational videos	InVideo AI Pictory VEED.IO Synthesia (limited), HeyGen	Flipped classroom, tutorials
	Infographics	Visual data representations	Piktochart AI Venngage MyMap.AI	Data visualisation
	Mind Maps	Concept mapping & brainstorming	MyMap.AI MindMap AI Algor Education Mapify	Study guides, planning
Assessment & feedback	Auto-Grading	AI essay & assignment grading	EssayGrader CoGrader Brisk Teaching Graded Pro	Teachers 6–12, University
	Feedback Generation	Personalised student feedback	Brisk Teaching Knowt AI FeedbackFruits	All teachers

(continued)

Table 3 (continued)

Category	*Subcategory*	*Description*	*Free/Accessible Tools*	*Best For*
	Rubric Generation	Create assessment rubrics	MagicSchool AI CoGrader Monsha Brisk Teaching	Teachers creating assessments
	Plagiarism Detection	Check originality & AI content	GPTZero Copyleaks Grammarly Scribbr	Teachers, students
	Progress Tracking	Monitor student learning	Khan Academy Dashboard Quizizz Analytics Google Classroom Insights	Teachers tracking progress
Gamification & engagement	Game Creation	Build educational games	Rosebud AI Eduaide.AI Just Think AI, Generic LLM	Teachers creating activities
	Interactive Quizzes	Competitive quiz platforms	Kahoot! Quizizz Genially Blooket	K-12, engagement
	Comprehensive LMS	Full gamified platforms	Coursebox AI Classcraft	Secondary, University
Writing assistance	Grammar Checking	Correct grammar & style	Grammarly LanguageTool QuillBot Scribbr	Students 6+, Teachers
	Paraphrasing	Rewrite & improve text	QuillBot Scribbr Paperpal	Academic writing
	Essay Writing	Academic writing support	Jenni AI Khan Academy Coach Paperpal	University students
	Citations	Generate bibliographies	MyBib QuillBot Scribbr Grammarly	All students

(continued)

Table 3 (continued)

Category	*Subcategory*	*Description*	*Free/Accessible Tools*	*Best For*
	Creative Writing	Story & creative content	Squibler CoWriter	Creative assignments
Personalised learning	AI Tutoring	One-on-one AI assistance	Khanmigo (Khan Academy) TutorOcean AI Socratic by Google Duolingo	Students K-12
	Adaptive Learning	Content adapts to student	Duolingo Khan Academy IXL (limited free)	Language, math learning
	Homework Help	Instant problem-solving	Photomath Symbolab Question AI StudyX	Math, science students
Accessibility	Speech-to-Text	Transcribe audio/lectures	Otter.ai TurboScribe Notta.ai	Lectures, meetings
	Auto-Subtitles	Generate video captions	VEED.IO HappyScribe EasySub	Video content
	Translation	Multilingual support	Google Translate Microsoft Translator	ESL, multilingual classes
	Text-to-Speech	Read text aloud	TTSReader NaturalReader Microsoft Immersive Reader	Accessibility, dyslexia
Research & synthesis	Summarisation	Condense long texts	Scribbr Summarizer Grammarly Paperpal NoteGPT	Research, study aids
	Research Assistants	Find academic sources	Elicit Consensus Semantic Scholar Perplexity AI	University research

(continued)

Table 3 (continued)

Category	*Subcategory*	*Description*	*Free/Accessible Tools*	*Best For*
	PDF Analysis	Chat with documents	ChatPDF SciSpace Copilot	Reading comprehension
	Note-Taking	AI-enhanced notes	Notion AI Otter.ai	Lecture notes
Coding & stem	Coding Tutors	Learn programming with AI	GitHub Copilot Replit AI Code.org Codecademy AI	Computer science students
	Math Solvers	Step-by-step math help	Photomath Symbolab Wolfram Alpha MathGPT	Math students K-12+
	STEM Multi-Subject	Broad STEM support	Question AI Khan Academy MagicSchool AI	Science, math, physics
	AI Learning Tools	Teach AI concepts	Teachable Machine ML for Kids AI for Oceans Quick, Draw!	Teaching about AI
Administrative tools	Lesson Planning	Create lesson plans	MagicSchool AI Curipod Brisk Teaching	Teachers planning
	LMS Integration	Connect with platforms	Google Classroom Canvas Free Schoology Basic	School admins
	Communication	Parent/admin communication	Magic School AI ChatGPT	Parent communication

- Gamification and engagement: AI-powered platforms support the creation of educational games, interactive quizzes, and comprehensive learning management systems that incorporate game-like elements. By leveraging competition, rewards, and interactive challenges, these tools can enhance student motivation and participation, particularly among younger learners.

- Writing assistance: AI provides comprehensive support for written communication, including grammar checking, paraphrasing, essay writing assistance, citation generation, and creative writing prompts. These tools help students develop their writing skills while reducing anxiety around composition and ensuring adherence to academic conventions.
- Personalised learning: AI enables one-on-one tutoring experiences, adaptive learning pathways that adjust to individual student performance, and instant homework help across various subjects. These applications embody the promise of truly differentiated instruction, responding in real time to each learner's pace, preferences, and proficiency level.
- Accessibility: AI technologies enhance educational equity by providing speech-to-text transcription, automatic subtitle generation, multilingual translation, and text-to-speech functionality. These tools remove barriers for students with disabilities, non-native speakers, and learners who benefit from multimodal content delivery.
- Research and synthesis: AI assists with academic research through text summarisation, identification of relevant scholarly sources, analysis of PDF documents, and AI-enhanced note-taking. These capabilities support students in navigating the overwhelming volume of information characteristic of contemporary knowledge environments.
- Coding and STEM: AI-powered tutors and problem solvers provide step-by-step guidance in programming, mathematics, and other STEM disciplines. Additionally, specialised tools designed to teach AI concepts themselves enable students to develop computational thinking and understand the technologies shaping their world.
- Administrative tools: AI supports teachers' organisational and communication responsibilities through lesson planning assistance, integration with learning management systems, and facilitation of parent-teacher communication. By automating routine administrative tasks, these tools free educators to focus on the relational and pedagogical dimensions of their work.

2 Methods and Tools

2.1 *The* Trial-and-Error *Technique to Understand How Machines Learn to Classify and Recognise*

How can we teach students the basic concepts of machine learning? How can we facilitate understanding of an AI model's learning processes? One instructional well suited to this purpose is *trial and error*, an approach that closely mirrors the learning methods typical of ML itself. Trial and error is grounded in the idea that knowledge is acquired through iterative cycles of attempts, mistakes, and subsequent corrections. Originally examined in the context of animal learning, it was later extended to human instruction and learning. Edward Thorndike, a pioneer in this field, described trial and error as a process of "selection and association," in which individuals solve problems through a series of attempts, selecting and associating those solutions that lead to a positive outcome (Thorndike, 1911). In this process, feedback and reinforcement are essential: behaviour is shaped by the consequences of each action. In other words, learners adjust future behaviour through direct experience of those consequences. One hallmark of the technique is direct experimentation, which not only makes the learning process more engaging but also allows students to confront the problem firsthand. Such active involvement helps learners develop practical skills and retain knowledge more effectively, since active involvement strengthens memory (EEF, 2014). Moreover, within the trial-and-error framework, errors themselves acquire formative value at the cognitive level. Every mistake, indeed, offers the opportunity to learn something new. Although the fear of making mistakes can be an obstacle to learning, discouraging students from exploring novel strategies or ideas, reframing mistakes as learning opportunities, encourages them to experiment and take intellectual risks, fostering deeper understanding and greater creativity.

Furthermore, trial and error prove particularly effective in promoting problem-solving skills: instead of supplying students with a ready-made answer, the teacher introduces the problem and encourages learners to discover a solution through experimentation.

Finally, the trial-and-error method favours student autonomy. Learners are not dependent on the teacher for every answer; rather, they are prompted to work out solutions independently, with positive effects on self-esteem and self-directed learning. In practice, adopting this technique enables students to refine their powers of discernment gradually and to gain familiarity with the categories and criteria needed to make precise distinctions.

Specifically, the trial-and-error technique can be deployed to help students understand how machines learn to classify and recognise. Indeed, classification is a quintessential supervised-learning task, in which the goal is to predict the category or class of an observation (James et al., 2013). To this purpose algorithms learn to classify and detect patterns through a process analogous to trial and error: they are trained on large datasets in which each observation carries a known class label, they generate predictions, and they correct their mistakes on the basis of the feedback. As the number of examples grows, the algorithm adapts and improves, becoming ever more accurate at recognising and classifying patterns in the data.

One illustrative application is teaching the biological classification of living organisms. Students first familiarise themselves with the principal taxonomic ranks: kingdom, phylum, class, order, family, genus, and species. They then examine a series of specimens and attempt to classify. Inevitably, mistakes occur, yet each error and the ensuing feedback provide an opportunity to learn and to refine classification skills. As students progress in their learning, they will be able to recognise and classify organisms with increasing accuracy and confidence. A variety of tools can support this process, including flashcards, interactive quizzes, game-based learning apps, and hands-on activities. For example, students may use flashcards to memorise characteristic features of different organisms; an interactive quiz can then test their classification skills and supply immediate feedback, enabling them to learn from mistakes and enhance recognition. Game-based learning apps make the process still more engaging by incorporating game mechanics that motivate learners and help them monitor their progress. Below, we present an example of a trial-and-error activity designed to teach mechanisms of recognition and classification. The activity can be adapted to different educational levels by adjusting its complexity accordingly.

"AI and the Oceans": Classifying with Trial and Error

Through this activity, students not only learn to reason about the characteristics that distinguish living organisms and to classify different species of fish, but they also experience firsthand the learning process of an ML algorithm. Most importantly, they discover that making mistakes is a fundamental part of learning—for both humans and machines.

Introduction

To begin, the teacher distributes cards bearing images of various items that might be found in the oceans: several species of fish, but also waste such as plastic bottles, aluminium cans, and plastic bags. Each student receives a set of cards to examine. In addition to the cards, the teacher provides a list of distinguishing characteristics such as "has scales," "is made of plastic," or "lives in water." The students' task is to use these characteristics both to differentiate fish from waste and to classify the distinct types of fish depicted on their cards.

Work Instructions

The teacher does not give explicit directions on how to apply the characteristics to perform the classification. Instead, students are allowed to navigate the task autonomously, exploring different strategies. As they begin to tackle the task, they inevitably encounter challenges and make mistakes. Some discover that the characteristics they first selected are not specific enough to differentiate between certain fish; others realise that some traits are more useful than others. Through this iterative process of trial and error, students gradually develop a deeper understanding of distinction and classification.

Reflection and Feedback

Once everyone has had the opportunity to experiment with various strategies, the teacher reconvenes the class for discussion. Students share the strategies they found effective and the characteristics that were most helpful. The teacher underscores how this learning process underscores that of a ML classification algorithm. Just as the students adjust their methods through trial and error, an ML classifier "learns" to distinguish categories by continually refining its parameters in response to results.

2.2 The Gamification Method to Understand How Machines Learn to Estimate and Predict

Another useful method for teaching key concepts of machine learning is gamification, specifically learning gamification, a pedagogical approach that integrates game mechanics into non-ludic contexts with the aim of increasing motivation, engagement and learning effectiveness (Kapp, 2012). Specifically, it involves applying elements customarily associated with games such as competition, rewards, progression, and narration, to domains not traditionally linked to play, including training and formal education (Deterding et al., 2011). Gamification seeks to leverage humans' innate affinity for play and competition to render learning a more engaging and motivating experience. Rather than presenting instruction as a mandatory task, it transforms it into a stimulating challenge that encourages students to participate actively, thereby generating a sense of competition and achievement (Zichermann and Cunningham, 2011).

Moreover, gamification favours an active learning stance: students are not mere spectators, but active protagonists who make decisions, solve problems and receive immediate feedback on their actions. As Gee (2007) observes, games can simulate authentic problem-solving contexts within a safe environment, enabling learners to apply newly acquired knowledge in practice.

The main characteristics of gamification can be summarised as follows (Kapp, 2012).

- **Game elements**. These form the fulcrum of gamification and include mechanics such as points, badges, leaderboards, objectives, missions, levels, and avatars. Such elements provide immediate feedback, set clear objectives, and create a sense of competition or cooperation among learners, thereby enhancing engagement and motivation.
- **Motivation and engagement**. By integrating game mechanics, gamification fosters feelings of competition, progress, and achievement, stimulating students' intrinsic motivation. Rewards and recognition further boost extrinsic motivation, tapping into the natural human drive to compete, reach goals, express oneself, and collaborate with others.
- **Active learning**. Gamification prompts students to take an active role in the learning process. Games create immersive environments that simulate real-world situations, enabling learners to apply and test what they have learned in a safe context.
- **Immediate feedback.** Mechanics such as scores, levels, and badges provide learners with instant feedback on their progress and performance, helping to sustain high levels of motivation.
- **Socialisation.** Many games incorporate social elements, including competition or cooperation with other players. Gamification can

leverage these features to promote collaborative learning and strengthen a sense of community.

The application of this method to AI literacy enables students to grasp how machines learn to estimate and predict (Huber et al., 2024). In essence, a prediction is a statement of what one believes will occur, grounded in contextual clues. A reader, for example, may predict aspects of a story by drawing on the title, the cover illustration, or earlier plot points. A typical classroom prompt asks students what they think a book is about based on the title and cover, or what might happen next after a partial reading.

Making predictions before and during a task is a vital component of building comprehension. Students use this strategy to connect prior knowledge to new information. As learners begin to use this strategy, they become more attentive to textual details and use them to inform their predictions. Moreover, by later evaluating those predictions, they gauge how well they have understood the text as a whole. In the context of ML, prediction refers to the model's ability—after training—to estimate an uncertain outcome based on previously observed data. The model interprets latent patterns within the data to produce meaningful outputs, most often in the form of classification or regression (Hastie et al., 2009). Whereas classification separates data into discrete categories, prediction (or regression) aims, instead, to approximate the underlying distribution so as to forecast future or unseen values (Dhar, 2013).

This learning-and-prediction cycle underpins many everyday technologies, from online product recommendations to text autocompletion on a search engine. Therefore, teaching the concept to younger students not only enriches their understanding of the technological landscape around them, but also—as the next chapter will show—lays the groundwork for a critical stance towards AI. In an era when AI-based decisions can affect fundamental aspects of society, the ability to evaluate, question, and contextualise AI's potentials and limitations is more crucial than ever.

Gamification can render the teaching of ML prediction engaging and intuitive, helping translate complex ideas into accessible learning experiences. Below, we present an example of an activity based on gamification and aimed at teaching mechanisms related to prediction. The exercise can be adapted to different educational levels by adjusting its complexity accordingly.

A Picnic in the Mountains: Predicting with Gamification

Through this activity, students are introduced to the concept of probability and prediction in ML, experiencing how models can be built and used to generate forecasts from available data.

Introduction

In a mountain village, there has been a significant increase in wild-animal sightings, and the class must determine which areas are safest for a picnic. Fortunately, the group has access to the list of sightings made in previous days in neighbouring villages. The teacher divides students into small teams and distributes a task card that describes the activity; the card also lists the characteristics of the various areas (for example, whether the space is outdoors or indoors, the type of location or structure, population density, noise level, and so forth) along with the number and type of wild animals observed. An empty column is provided for each team's prediction. Based on the information supplied, students must estimate (by comparing similar areas, averaging counts, etc.) the probability of encountering wild animals in a particular village location designated by the teacher. Teams then compare their predictions with the ground-truth figures (prepared in advance by the teacher). Each accurate prediction earns one point, and the team with the highest score at the end wins the game.

Work Instructions

Students first examine the dataset showing how many animals have been sighted in different village areas and record their observations, including notes on any "similarities" they discern among areas and patterns within the data. The teacher may simplify or complicate the game by revealing—or withholding—the specific features used to generate the sighting counts. Students might notice, for example, that certain animals avoid noisy zones and favour outdoor spaces. They might also observe that animals tend to group in places where people or food are present such as picnic sites or refreshment areas. The activity can include optional "missions" of escalating difficulty, each with higher rewards (e.g., badges or leader-board points).

Final reflection and feedback in a plenary session, teams justify the basis of their scores, for example by citing animal behaviours or the similarity between areas but also reflect on what an inaccurate prediction could signify, as well as the potential impacts of erroneous forecasts in real-world contexts.

References

AI HLEG (High-Level Expert Group on Artificial Intelligence) (2019), *Ethics Guidelines for Trustworthy AI*, European Commission, Brussels.

Allen, L. K., Graesser, A. C., & McNamara, D. S. (2023). *Automated analyses of natural language in psychological research.* In G. G. H. R. Schütze (Eds.), *The Oxford handbook of computational and digital psychology.* Oxford University Press.

Barocas S. *et al.* (2017), *The problem with bias: Allocative versus representational harms in machine learning*, in 9th Annual Conference of the Special Interest Group for Computing, Information and Society (Mountain view, CA, March 18–19, 2017)

Bender, E. M., Gebru, T., McMillan-Major, A., & Shmitchell, S. (2021), *On the dangers of stochastic parrots: Can language models be too big?* In Proceedings of the 2021 ACM Conference on Fairness, Accountability, and Transparency (pp. 610–623). Association for Computing Machinery.

Bishop C.M. (2006), *Pattern Recognition and Machine learning*, Springer, New York, NY.

Boden, M. A. (2016). *AI: Its Nature and Future.* Oxford University Press, Oxford.

Brown, T., Mann, B., Ryder, N., Subbiah, M., Kaplan, J. D., Dhariwal, P., ... & Amodei, D. (2020). *Language models are few-shot learners. Advances in neural information processing systems*, *33*, 1877–1901.

Chowdhery, A. *et al.* (2023). *PaLM: Scaling language modeling with pathways. Journal of Machine Learning Research*, 24(240), 1–113.

Deterding, S. *et al.* (2011), *From game design elements to gamefulness: defining gamification* in Proceedings of the 15th International Academic MindTrek Conference: Envisioning Future Media Environments (Tampere, Finland, 28–30 2011), Association for Computing Machinery, New York, NY.

Devlin, J., Chang, M. W., Lee, K., & Toutanova, K. (2019). *Bert: Pre-training of deep bidirectional transformers for language understanding.* In Proceedings of the 2019 conference of the North American chapter of the association for computational linguistics: human language technologies, volume 1 (long and short papers) (pp. 4171–4186).

Dhar V. (2013), *Data science and prediction*, in Communications of the ACM, 56(12), pp. 64–73.

Education Endowment Foundation. (2014, February). *Switch-on Reading: Evaluation report and executive summary*. https://files.eric.ed.gov/fulltext/ED581466.pdf

Gee J. P. (2007), *What Video Games Have to Teach Us About Learning and Literacy*, Palgrave Macmillan, New York, NY.

Goodfellow I. *et al.* (2014), *Generative Adversarial Nets* in Advances in Neural Information Processing Systems, 27, pp. 1–9.

Hastie T. *et al.* (2009), *The elements of statistical learning: data mining, inference, and prediction,* Springer, New York, NY (2nd ed.).

Huber, S. E., Kiili, K., Nebel, S., et al. (2024*). Leveraging the potential of large language models in education through playful and game-based learning*. Educational Psychology Review, 36(1), 25. https://doi.org/10.1007/s10648-024-09868-z

James, G., Witten, D., Hastie, T., & Tibshirani, R. (2013). *An introduction to statistical learning: with applications in R* (Vol. 103). New York: springer.

Jobin A., Ienca M., Vayena E. (2019), *The global landscape of AI ethics guidelines* in "Nature Machine Intelligence," 1(9), pp. 389–99.

Jordan M. I., Mitchell T. M. (2015), *Machine learning: Trends, perspectives, and prospects*, in "Science," 349(6245), pp. 255–60.

Kapp K.M. (2012), *The Gamification of Learning and Instruction: Game-based Methods and Strategies for Training and Education*, Pfeiffer, San Francisco, CA.

Maity, S., & Deroy, A. (2024). *Generative ai and its impact on personalized intelligent tutoring systems*. arXiv preprint arXiv:2410.10650.

McClelland J. L., Rumelhart D. E., Hinton G. E. (1986), *The appeal of parallel distributed processing*, in Rumelhart D. E., McClelland J. L., the PDP Research Group (eds.), *Parallel distributed processing: Explorations in the microstructure of cognition*, vol I, Cambridge, MA, MIT Press, pp. 3–44.

McCulloch W.S., Pitts W. (1943), *A logical calculus of the ideas immanent in nervous activity*, in "Bulletin of Mathematical Biophysics," 5, pp. 115–33.

Miao F., Holmes W. (2021), *AI and education: Guidance for policy-makers*, UNESCO, (https://unesdoc.unesco.org/ark:/48223/pf0000376709).

Minsky, M., & Papert, S. A. (1969). *Perceptrons: An introduction to computational geometry*. MIT Press.

Nye, B. D. (2015). *Intelligent tutoring systems by and for the developing world: A review of trends and approaches for educational technology in a global context. International Journal of Artificial Intelligence in Education*, 25(2), 177–203.

Ouyang, L. *et al.* (2022). *Training language models to follow instructions with human feedback.* In *Advances in Neural Information Processing Systems* 35 (pp. 27730–27744). Curran Associates, Inc.

Pavlik, P. I., Brawner, K., Olney, A., & Mitrovic, A. (2013). *A review of student models used in intelligent tutoring systems*. In R. A. Sottilare, A. C. Graesser, X. Hu, & A. M. Sinatra (Eds.), *Design recommendations for intelligent tutoring systems: Vol. 1. Learner modeling* (pp. 39–68). U.S. Army Research Laboratory.

Perrotta C. (2022), *Advancing data justice in education: Some suggestions toward a deontological framework*, in Learning, Media and Technology, 1–13.

Radford, A., Narasimhan, K., Salimans, T., & Sutskever, I. (2018). *Improving language understanding by generative pre-training*. OpenAI.

Radford, A., Wu, J., Child, R., Luan, D., Amodei, D., & Sutskever, I. (2019). *Language models are unsupervised multitask learners*. OpenAI Blog.

Ramesh, A. *et al.* (2021). *Zero-shot text-to-image generation*. In *Proceedings of the 38th International Conference on Machine Learning* (Vol. 139, pp. 8821–8831). PMLR.

Rosenblatt F. (1962), *Principles of Neurodynamics: Perceptrons and the Theory of Brain Mechanisms*, Spartan Books, Washington DC.

Russell S. J., Norvig P. (2009), *Artificial intelligence: a modern approach*, Prentice Hall, Upper Saddle River, NJ.

Thorndike E. L. (1911), *Animal intelligence: Experimental studies*, Macmillan Press, New York, NY.

Touvron, H. *et al.* (2023). *Llama 2: Open foundation and fine-tuned chat models* [Preprint]. arXiv.

UNESCO (2021). *AI and Education: Guidance for Policymakers*, (https://unesdoc.unesco.org/ark: /48223/pf0000376709).

Vaswani, A. *et al.* (2017). *Attention is all you need*. In *Advances in Neural Information Processing Systems* 30 (NIPS 2017) (pp. 5998–6008). Curran Associates, Inc.

Wright, A. (2024). *Worldwide IDC global datasphere forecast, 2024–2028: Ai everywhere, but upsurge in data will take time*. International Data Corporation.

Yim, I. H. Y., & Su, J. (2025). *Artificial intelligence (AI) learning tools in K-12 education: A scoping review*. Journal of Computers in Education, 12(1), 93–131. https://doi.org/10.1007/s40692-023-00304-9

Zawacki-Richter, O., Marín, V. I., Bond, M., & Gouverneur, F. (2019). *Systematic review of research on artificial intelligence applications in higher education–where are the educators? International Journal of Educational Technology in Higher Education*, 16(1), 1–27.

Zichermann G., Cunningham C. (2011), *Gamification by Design: Implementing Game Mechanics in Web and Mobile Apps*, O'Reilly Media, Sebastopol, CA.

The Critical Dimension: Understanding and Evaluation Beyond Automation

Abstract This chapter investigates the critical dimension of Artificial Intelligence Literacy, focusing on the evaluation of AI systems and their outputs. It first outlines the primary challenges to critical understanding, beginning with the need for advanced data and information literacy to navigate the risks inherent in generative AI—such as bias, misinformation, and hallucinations. It then examines the *black-box* problem, establishing explainable AI (XAI) and user-centred techniques like Chain-of-Thought (CoT) prompting as fundamental conditions for trust and accountability. To address these challenges, this chapter proposes two corresponding pedagogical strategies. To foster critical information use, it details an Inquiry-Based Learning (IBL) approach that turns tools like ChatGPT into objects of critical investigation. To demystify AI's internal logic and decision-making, it presents a Problem-Based Learning (PBL) framework, employing practical activities such as error analysis and the construction of simple decision trees. This chapter concludes that these hands-on, inquiry-driven methods are essential for moving learners from passive consumption to active, critical, and responsible engagement with AI technologies.

Keywords Bias, misinformation, hallucinations · Information & data literacy · Explainability (XAI) · Critical investigation · Building decision trees

M. Ranieri et al., *Artificial Intelligence in Schools*, Digital Education and Learning, https://doi.org/10.1007/978-3-032-15919-9_4

1 Themes and Issues

1.1 Data & Information Literacy in the Age of AI

One of the main consequences of the digitalisation of our societies—as already pointed out—is the uncontrollable proliferation of data (Borgman, 2016). The ongoing digital infrastructuring of our informational, cognitive, educational, communicative, recreational, and other activities is producing an unprecedented phenomenon: the generation of enormous quantities of data created by human action within platforms (Van Dijck, 2014).

Two expressions are commonly used to describe these new phenomena: *platformisation* and *datafication*—both of which are further amplified by the development of Artificial Intelligence (AI) technologies (Perrotta et al., 2021). The former, platformisation, is defined as "the penetration of the infrastructures, economic processes, and governmental frameworks of platforms in different economic sectors and spheres of life. [...] we conceive this process as the reorganisation of cultural practices and imaginations around platforms" (Poell et al., 2019, pp. 5–6).

The second, datafication, refers to the process through which digital platforms translate into data practices and activities that have historically escaped quantification (Van Dijck, 2014). This encompasses not only demographic and profiling data voluntarily disclosed by users, but—above all—behavioural metadata, collected via apps, plug-ins, active and passive sensors, trackers, and devices now embedded in everyday technologies such as smartphones, thereby transforming virtually any human interaction into data. These are processed algorithmically and, under certain circumstances, made available—often unpredictably and without user control—to a wide variety of external actors. Another way to characterise this socio-technical metamorphosis is through the expression *platform society* (Van Dijck et al., 2018).

It is no coincidence that in May 2017 *The Economist* proclaimed data as the world's most valuable resource: "Data is the new oil" has become the battle cry of modern organisations because, just as oil fuelled economic growth in the twentieth century, data will catalyse growth in the twenty-first.

In parallel, recent advances in AI systems have been enabled—among other factors—by this unprecedented availability of vast amounts of data. The trajectories of datafication and platformisation intersect with that of AI at multiple levels, particularly in machine learning (ML), which trains on data to generate intelligent behaviours—or, as we saw earlier (see chapter "The Cognitive Dimension: Historical Framework and Basic Concepts"), behaviours indistinguishable from those a human might produce.

Crucial, then, is reflecting on the concept of *data* in order to understand how these systems function and evaluate their implications for individuals and society. Attention to data—for the reasoning proposed in this section—is driven by a twofold interest: on the one hand, as active users of AI technologies, we cannot rely on such systems to make decisions on often sensitive matters without clear awareness of the complexity associated with the digital data collection and generation; on the other hand, as passive users of AI technologies or, more broadly, as consumers of digital media and technologies, we cannot ignore the issues surrounding the acquisition and use of data that affect us.

All this presupposes competences associated with data literacy (Ghodoosi et al., 2023), a new literacy increasingly linked to the notion of digital competence and instrumental for developing AI literacy from the perspective of critical and informed use of AI systems. The subject, as one might expect, is highly complex. Let us begin, however, with a simple question: What is data?

Following Borgman's (2016, p. xviii) definition, "[…] data *rarely* are things at all. They are not natural objects with an essence of their own. Rather, data are representations of observations, objects, or other entities used as evidence of phenomena for the purposes of research or scholarship. Those representations vary by scholar, circumstance, and over time. Across the sciences, social sciences, and the humanities, scholars create, use, analyze, and interpret data, often without agreeing on what those data are." And again, "Data exist in a context, taking on meaning from that context and from the perspective of the beholder" (ibid., p. 18). This definition immediately dispels the illusion that data can be something objective. Data are not born neutral; the risk that they may contain or reflect stereotypes and prejudices is intrinsic to their very constitution. Since there has been a proliferation of data collection and processing systems beyond citizens' control—despite their being the recipients of the multiple products, services, and interventions built upon them—this knowledge vacuum harbours several risks. This is why there is increasing talk of (critical) data literacy education as a pedagogical tool to develop new forms of citizenship capable of acknowledging and addressing the challenges of the data society (Pangrazio and Selwyn, 2023). Obviously, the problem cannot be solved at the educational and individual level alone; regulatory interventions appropriate to the complexity of governing a process already far advanced in its development are needed. Nevertheless, attributing to literacy the power of emancipation (Freire, 1970), we dwell on this new competence to outline its contours in relation to AI.

In this regard, it should first be noted that we have moved from an initial conception strongly linked to computational and statistical traditions to a later view that interprets data literacy as a fundamental prerequisite for proactive participation in the platform society. According to Carmi et al. (2020), for example, data literacy is a new competence required not only for work, personal development, and social inclusion, but also for cultivating citizens' awareness of the cultural, political, social, and economic implications of the progressive datafication of our societies. Related to this, the authors speak of data citizenship exercised at three levels: (i) *data thinking*—the critical reading, collection, and understanding of data by citizens; (ii) *data doing*—actions that can be actively undertaken, such as requesting the deletion of personal data and using acquired data in an ethical manner; and (iii) *data participation*—indicating proactive engagement in forms of civic activism and support for the spread of data literacy. Similarly, Bhargava and D'Ignazio (2015) defined data literacy as the acquisition of skills extending beyond purely technical-mathematical competences: on the one hand, the ability to read, create, interpret, and manage data; on the other hand, a critical dimension that entails understanding aspects of reality represented through transformation into informational units, as well as the capacity to sustain, via data, a broader narrative aimed at communicating a specific message to a particular audience. With a specific focus on personal data, Pangrazio and Selwyn (2023) discuss critical data literacy, namely critical personal-data management skills encompassing five aspects: *data identification* (understanding the type of data, e.g., whether voluntarily surrendered or automatically extracted by the system); *understanding the data* (how it is handled and processed); *data reflexivity* (analysing the implications of personal-data reuse); *critical use of data* (e.g., reading the Terms of Service, managing privacy settings); and *the tactical use* of data from a civic-activism perspective.

Mapping these competences onto the terrain of AI, we can say that data thinking (Carmi et al., 2020) is fundamental when using data to make decisions supported by automated systems. Consider the following example: as teachers, we may wish to locate supplementary resources for a particular topic. We might consult several online repositories and examine peer reviews, using those data to inform our choice of materials for students. At this level, we determine which data sources are needed and how to collect and apply them. Data doing (Carmi et al., 2020)—or critical data literacy (Pangrazio and Selwyn, 2023)—becomes essential when we deploy AI technologies that covertly capture personal data. Critical literacy here is required to mitigate risks associated with abusive third-party extraction and exploitation of such data.

The landscape has recently grown even more complex with the explosion of generative AI (see chapter "The Operational Dimension: Uses and Applications"), particularly AI-powered chatbots such as OpenAI's ChatGPT, Google's Gemini, Meta's LLaMA, Anthropic's Claude. These applications rely on Large Language Models (LLMs) capable of producing text on an almost limitless range of topics. Their ability to mine massive datasets, extract latent patterns, and deliver seemingly relevant and accurate responses has triggered fear, uncertainty, and doubt—especially in educational and academic contexts. As Schmarzo (2023, p. 173) observes, "Yes, ChatGPT changed everything by elevating the critical importance of AI and data literacy to the forefront of global priorities overnight." ChatGPT (where GPT stands for Generative Pre-trained Transformer) is a chatbot based on generative AI, an automated learning paradigm designed to create original digital content (e.g., articles, programming code, poems, photographs, artwork and music, summaries, translations) by learning from existing data. Faced with user prompts, ChatGPT delivers automated assistance in natural-language prose that incorporates data and information drawn from its training corpus. In a sense, we can say that this application is changing our relationship with digital information, as it mediates between information seekers and information sources. One of the main concerns regarding the use of these systems is that, in practice, we do not yet know all their possible areas of application: the potential of generative AI has yet to be fully explored.

Nevertheless, there are some known risks that can be monitored in design, development, and implementation, namely (ibid.):

- **Confirmation bias.** In psychology, this term denotes a cognitive bias whereby people assimilate new experiences within the scope of their pre-existing beliefs. AI systems can exacerbate confirmation bias in human users who rely on their outputs, negatively affecting areas such as lending and finance, housing, employment, criminal justice, and healthcare—an even more serious issue given that the systems themselves are not free from biases present in the data (see Sect. 1.3 in chapter "The Operational Dimension: Uses and Applications").

- **Unintended consequences.** These are the unforeseen outcomes of an action or decision. They should be mitigated by involving a diverse group of stakeholders in assessing the potential negative and positive consequences of AI implementations.
- **Mental atrophy**. This refers to the gradual decline in the effectiveness of our mental abilities due to cognitive delegation to the medium. We need to continue to challenge our thinking to keep our cognitive capacities active.
- **Hallucinations**. These occur when the generative AI model produces nonsensical, misleading, or entirely fabricated outputs, leading to unreliable and potentially harmful information. Such hallucinations can contribute to the spread of false information, erosion of trust in AI, ethical concerns, legal liabilities, and social manipulation. It is crucial to understand that hallucinations are not a temporary flaw but an inherent feature of the current LLM architecture, and while they can be reduced, they are unlikely to be eliminated completely. This is due to two core reasons. First, these models are fundamentally probabilistic sequence predictors, not databases of facts. Their goal is to generate a statistically plausible continuation of a text, not to verify truth. If a fabricated statement is grammatically correct and statistically likely based on the training data, the model can generate it with high confidence. Second, an LLM's "knowledge" is a form of lossy compression of vast amounts of text into a finite set of parameters. The model does not store facts discretely but learns statistical relationships between words. When retrieving information, it reconstructs it from these patterns, a process that can easily introduce errors, blend concepts, or invent details, much like a human misremembering a story. This inherent architectural trait makes human verification and critical evaluation non-negotiable skills when interacting with these systems.
- **Intellectual property protection**. The debate concerns the ownership and control of content created by generative AI, as well as the potential risks associated with data exposure and accidental

disclosure of sensitive information, including trade secrets. Content creators such as authors and artists fear losing control over their original works and not being adequately compensated for unauthorised use or infringement of intellectual property by these systems.

In this scenario, not only data literacy but also information literacy is crucial. In 2016, the Association of College and Research Libraries (ACRL) proposed new standards that emphasise the contextual and socially constructed nature of the process of information construction and use with reference to authorship (in that information reflects the expertise and credibility of its creators and is valued according to the information needs and the context in which it will be used); to information creation as a process (i.e., information in any format is produced to convey a message and is shared through a certain mode of delivery); to the value of information (as a commercially exchangeable commodity, as an educational tool, and as a means of influencing and negotiating understanding of the world); to research as inquiry (i.e., as an iterative process in which questions generate answers that generate questions); to scholarship as conversation (which engages communities of scholars and practitioners in comparing various perspectives and interpretations); and to searching as strategic exploration (in that it requires the evaluation of a range of sources and the mental flexibility to pursue alternative avenues).

These skills lay the foundation for the critical use of generative AI systems: confirmation bias is countered by information seeking, understood as a recursive process aimed at expanding boundaries rather than confirming them; mental atrophy is overcome through information seeking conceived as strategic exploration that requires comparing sources and pursuing alternative avenues; hallucinations are mitigated through active dialogue with colleagues and the relevant community, and so on. As we shall see later (see Sect. 4.2.1), building educational activities that leverage these aspects is one way to cultivate critical skills required to employ systems of this nature.

1.2 Explainability as a Fundamental Condition for a Critical Approach to AI

As we saw in chapter "The Operational Dimension: Uses and Applications", machine learning (ML), an integral part of AI, is a rapidly evolving field, transforming several sectors of our society. However, despite its impressive progress, it faces challenges inherent in its very nature and application, ranging from the problem of bias and fairness to the role of data (the quality of which, both in terms of accuracy and representativeness, is crucial, since a model can only be as good as the data on which it is trained), to scalability and computational efficiency (which requires a lot of energy with environmental implications), to the security and robustness of models, and finally to privacy. Among these challenges—which will be the subject of the next chapter—we focus here on the issues of interpretability and transparency of models, these being fundamental requirements for an informed approach to AI. Indeed, as algorithms grow more complex, it becomes increasingly difficult to understand how they make decisions and to answer questions about decision responsibility and the possibility of corrective action (O'Neil, 2016).

It may seem counterintuitive that an algorithm could be unclear or unexplained, so clarification is needed: within the symbolic approach, algorithms operate primarily as engines of logical inference, following well-defined rules and processes to reach conclusions and explicit knowledge representations. Algorithms in this context are often clear and interpretable because they are deterministic, functioning as a set of programmed instructions (see chapter "The Operational Dimension: Uses and Applications"). By contrast, in the machine learning approach, and even more so in deep learning, algorithms operate differently. Rather than following fixed rules, they learn from large amounts of data, adapting their internal structures to identify patterns and relationships hidden in the data itself. The exact nature of how they work can be much more difficult to interpret, since they do not follow a linear, predetermined path to reach a solution but continually adapt based on the data they receive, adjusting their weights through the process of backpropagation described earlier (see Sect. 1.1 in chapter "The Operational Dimension: Uses and Applications"). Consequently, as ML techniques become increasingly sophisticated, many of the models underlying the latest AI applications take on a black-box characteristic—that is, while they provide very accurate predictions or decisions, they do so in ways that are difficult to interpret or understand.

This is a particularly significant problem when they are used in sensitive areas such as medicine, education, or law, where decisions can have a major impact on people's lives. In all these contexts, there is often a lack of what the industry refers to as *explainability*, a key concept in AI denoting the capacity to render a model's decision-making processes understandable and interpretable to humans (Ribeiro et al., 2016). This absence can lead to incorrect, unfair, or discriminatory decisions. Consider, for example, an ML model in the medical domain aimed at diagnosing diseases. If it produces erroneous diagnoses, the consequences may be severe both in the case of an undiagnosed condition and in that of a "false positive"—certainly less serious, yet still impactful in terms of the patient's psychological stress and the explicit and sunk costs for the healthcare system, including possible delays for other important diagnoses.

This challenge of opacity is so central that new methods are emerging not just at the technical level, but also in terms of user interaction. A prominent example is *Chain-of-Thought* (CoT) prompting (Wei et al., 2022). By simply instructing a model to "think step-by-step" before providing a final answer, the model is encouraged to externalise a sequence of putative "reasoning." This yields a semblance of transparency: while the internal workings of the neural network remain a black box, the generated reasoning path can be inspected, evaluated, and debugged by a human user.

This development, further refined in recent models explicitly designed for complex reasoning, does not amount to true technical explainability; it does not reveal why the model chose one step over another at a probabilistic level. Nevertheless, it represents a powerful, practical bridge. It mitigates the black-box problem from the outside in, making the model's conclusions less opaque and more trustworthy, and turning the interaction itself into a site for critical evaluation.

But the issue extends far beyond the model's ability to make accurate diagnoses. Even with high accuracy, it would be potentially dangerous if physicians did not understand the logic underlying its outputs. The ML model, regardless of its accuracy, remains a tool—and like any tool, its true value is determined by its practical use, guided by the human expert. Continuing with the example, physicians, with their experience and knowledge, must be able to examine and interpret the results within the patient's specific clinical context. Indeed, in many situations, medical decisions are not simply binary and require in-depth analysis. This makes explainability not only desirable but essential, allowing the model's reliability to be assessed, the entire decision-making process to be monitored, and, if necessary, informed action to be taken. It follows that one of the main challenges is the trade-off between accuracy and explainability. In general, largely for reasons related to computational load, the most accurate models tend to be the most complex, and therefore the most difficult to explain and interpret. By contrast, simpler models are more transparent and understandable but typically provide lower accuracy. How this trade-off is managed depends greatly on the specific context. In some situations, such as medicine or law, it may be more important to have an explainable model than a highly precise one (so that the practitioners are able to recognise and intervene if distortions arise). Conversely, in other cases, such as in forecasting weather events, accuracy might be more important than explainability.

The importance of context also relates to the fact that different people may need diverse types of explanations, depending on their background, goals, and level of familiarity with ML. For instance, an engineer might be interested in understanding the inner workings of the model, while a physician might be more interested in knowing which variables had the greatest impact on a particular decision. This means that there is no "one size fits all" for explainability and that explanations must be tailored to specific audiences, as this generates benefits not only for end users but also for the developers of such models. Indeed, explainability not only provides insight into how the model uses input characteristics to make predictions or decisions but can also reveal any biases in the data or decisions (see Sect. 1.2 in chapter "The Operational Dimension: Uses and Applications") that might otherwise go unnoticed.

The explainability of artificial intelligence, often discussed in purely technical terms, is a key component of a broader human-centric approach that aims to build trustworthy AI (AI HLEG, 2019; Nazaretsky et al., 2025). This concept is clearly expressed in the Transparency section (see chapter "The Ethical Dimension: General Principles and Educational Proposals") of the European AI Guidelines, where the importance of traceability of these systems is emphasised. It is essential not only to record and document the decisions made by the systems, but also the entire process that led to those decisions, including the collection and labelling of the data, and the description of the algorithm used.

Although explainability is a concept of growing importance, implementing it is not an easy task, especially with more complex machine learning models (Doshi-Velez and Kim, 2017). There are several methods used to improve the explainability of models. These methods can be divided into two main categories: intrinsic methods and post-hoc methods (Adadi and Berrada, 2018).

Intrinsic methods involve the use of models that are "naturally" interpretable. For example, decision trees, linear and logistic regression, and generalised linear models are all inherently interpretable models because the relationship between input and output variables can be easily understood and explained. Using these models, we can obtain a clear explanation of how decisions or predictions are made. An inherently explainable model is, therefore, a machine learning model that offers transparency in its decisions by having a structure that allows its internal processes to be easily interpreted. For example, a decision tree, one of the most common models in this category, organises data through a series of questions or conditions. The structure of the tree consists of a series of bifurcations where, at each node, a specific question is asked (e.g., "Is characteristic X greater than Y?") and, based on the answer, the corresponding branch is followed until a leaf of the tree is reached that represents the final decision of the model.

The comprehensibility of the decision tree lies in its visualisation. We can literally trace a path from the root node to the last leaf node to understand clearly how the model arrived at a particular decision. In technical terms, we might say that an inherently explainable model is one in which the relationship between the input variables and the final decision can be clearly delineated and understood.

In practice, however, many of the latest AI applications use models, such as deep neural networks, with thousands, if not millions, of parameters contributing to the decision-making process, making it difficult, if not impossible, to understand the logic directly. The methods used to interpret this type of model are called *post-hoc* methods. They are applied after the model has been trained, in order to provide explanations for the decisions or predictions made. Post-hoc techniques include LIME (Local Interpretable Model-agnostic Explanations) and SHAP (SHapley Additive exPlanations), which attempt to explain model outputs by perturbing the input and evaluating the importance of each feature in the final prediction (Lundberg and Lee, 2017; Türkmen, 2025). For example, if we are trying to determine which characteristic was most influential in influencing a student's risk of dropping out, a LIME analysis will display—along with the prediction percentages -the weighted contribution of the features selected by the model. We may, therefore, find that the prediction was driven by the student's having missed many online sessions in the first few weeks or by a lack of participation in discussion forums. This explanation not only helps us understand the system's prediction but also offers insights into how we might intervene to support the student, surfacing signals that might otherwise have gone unnoticed by the teacher. Similarly, if we are dealing with a weather-forecasting model and want to understand how it predicted rain for the next day, LIME will create many alternatives "tomorrow"—some cloudy, some sunny and some windy—and then query the model for the forecast output for each scenario. By observing how the predictions change, LIME can make explicit which factors carry greater relevance for the model—whether, for example, clouds cover or wind. In this way, we can see how, from many hypothetical questions, a complex model arrives at its decisions, allowing us to conclude: "The rainfall forecast was mainly based on the presence of clouds."

These explainability methods are not only tools for engineers or researchers designing ML (Arrieta et al., 2020; Feldman-Maggor et al., 2025); they can also be deployed as teaching instruments in the classroom. In education, it is especially important that teachers and students clearly understand not only how these technologies work, but also how they can be used critically and responsibly.

In the classroom, clarity and understanding are paramount. Teachers strive to render complex concepts intelligible, while students seek to practise and reflect on what they learn. If we integrate AI as an educational support, it must operate according to the same principles. Education is more than the transfer of information; it is a formative course that elicits reflection, comprehension, and the development of a critical stance. If an AI system provides an answer or suggests a solution, students should be able to understand how and why that response was generated—or at least to be aware of the limitations and constraints shaping it. Through explainability, students can use AI not merely as a problem solver but as a catalyst for deep reflection.

We can therefore say that the ability to analyse and evaluate AI critically depends on our capacity to understand its processes. When students and teachers can examine the reasons why a model reaches a particular conclusion, they gain the opportunity to assess its effectiveness, biases, and potential implications. Such analysis, in turn, fosters a deeper understanding of the intersections among technology, society, and the individual.

Moreover, the introduction of AI into classrooms concerns not only students. Teachers, as mediators between technology and learning, must also possess a clear grasp of AI's underlying processes. Only with this clarity can they integrate it effectively into the curriculum, ensuring that it complements rather than displaces traditional pedagogy.

Specifically, with reference to the challenges noted earlier, teachers can explain the trade-off between accuracy and explainability, illustrate the importance of context in ML explanations, and discuss with students about the limitations of data-driven interpretations. For example, a teacher might use a decision tree to demonstrate how the model works, then interrogate its decisions by asking students to reflect on the variables the model deems important and how they are weighted in the output; alternatively, they might employ a heat map—a graphical representation highlighting how different features contribute to a model's decision—to cultivate more critical understanding.

In addition, teachers can design practical exercises and case studies to help students engage with these challenges. Activities might include discussing what it means for an ML model to be explainable, why explainability matters, and how it can be evaluated.

2 Methods and Tools

2.1 *ChatGPT as a Training Ground for Critical Thinking: An Inquiry-Based Learning Approach*

AI, in the form of advanced LLMs such as ChatGPT, has opened new frontiers in the world of information and communication. However, as we pointed out above, this progress is not without challenges, particularly with regard to critical-thinking training. Exclusive dependence on automated sources could, in fact, undermine our ability to analyse, evaluate, and contextualise information—an issue that is especially pressing in educational settings.

Since the emergence of Wikipedia, teachers' and educators' concerns about the casual use of online information have progressively increased: from "copy and paste" practice to the absence of critical evaluation and original reworking, educational systems have for years been confronted with the challenge of curbing modes of information consumption that verge on intellectual plagiarism. The explosion of ChatGPT has further exacerbated such concerns, as this chatbot not only draws on vast numbers of sources but also manages to aggregate and repackage them in a seemingly original way. Hence, the global proliferation of bans on the use of ChatGPT at the school and university level (García-Peñalvo, 2023).

Nevertheless, it would be a mistake to assume that merely entering any prompt into the system is sufficient to obtain high-quality output (Chatterjee and Dethlefs, 2023). In other words, there is a way—and a better way—to talk to the machine; a way—and a better way—to interact with it; and a way—and a better way—to collaborate with it. For example, it is one thing to use a prompt such as "Write an essay on the Industrial Revolution, illustrating its causes and effects" and to accept passively the response received; it is quite another to refine that response through iterative dialogue based on verification prompts such as: "Cite the sources you used to write your essay and rank them according to their reliability on a scale from 0 to 10. For each score, make explicit the criteria behind your evaluation and their application to the specific source." The simulation of an intelligent conversation with the machine could continue indefinitely.

This small example, however, highlights how the manner of questioning the machine can make a difference. What we find interesting is not so much the output that ChatGPT produces in terms of reusable intellectual or creative products, but the fact that systems of this kind can help us train and develop our own—and thus our students'—capacity to formulate questions (Lo, 2023).

In a short essay from the early 2000s, Ferraris (2003) described the Web as a training ground for learning to ask questions; today we can look to ChatGPT and similar applications as environments in which we can learn to become *expert prompters*, that is, practitioners skilled in giving instructions to the machine aimed at knowledge construction (and all that this entails in terms of reflexivity and critical thinking) in a world where knowledge is increasingly distributed between humans and technology. Understanding this is crucial to moving beyond prohibition perspectives on AI chatbots, fostering in students a greater awareness in the use of AI applications and turning ChatGPT into a pedagogical ally for cultivating reflective skills in the critical use of information.

A useful teaching approach for this purpose is Inquiry-Based Learning (IBL), or learning by discovery, which combines metacognitive and exploratory dimensions. This technique leverages the process of knowledge discovery based on the formulation and verification of hypotheses, engaging students in knowledge-building activities through the so-called inquiry cycle (Pedaste et al., 2015). The latter is structured into five phases: (i) an initial phase introducing the topic-problem (*Orientation*),

(ii) a question-generation phase, followed by web-based information searching and the formulation of initial hypotheses for solving the problem (*Conceptualisation*), (iii) an inquiry phase characterised by exploration, experimentation, and data interpretation (*Investigation*), (iv) a concluding phase in which the solution hypothesis is elaborated (*Conclusion*); and, lastly, (v) a final phase in which the identified solutions are communicated, shared, and evaluated (Discussion).

An inquiry-based teaching activity using ChatGPT, aimed at nurturing awareness in the use of AI applications by promoting critical skills in handling information resources, could be articulated as follows:

Step 1: Familiarising with ChatGPT

Students first familiarise themselves with ChatGPT, understanding what it is and how interaction with this application functions (*Orientation*). Following an initial general presentation by the teacher, students work in pairs to initiate a conversation with the chatbot by sending specific instructions. They read the responses, comment on them, and evaluate the quality of the interaction. If unsatisfied, and under the teacher's guidance, they refine the instructions until they achieve an appropriate conversational level. This initial activity emphasises the active role of the user: if one cannot formulate appropriate requests, satisfactory answers will not be obtained.

Step 2: Generating Text with ChatGPT

After initial familiarisation, students are organised into groups. The objective is to solve a problem introduced by the teacher, using ChatGPT both as an information-seeking and compilation tool. This involves formulating question-prompts and initial solution hypotheses (*Conceptualisation*). The outcomes of the conversations will differ across groups depending on the instructions provided. At the end of the activity, groups compare the texts generated by their queries to identify similarities and differences, reflecting on the diversity (or otherwise) of the prompts that produced those results (*Investigation*).

Step 3: Putting ChatGPT to the Test

Subsequent to the plenary discussion the groups return to the text generated in their ChatGPT interaction to assess its quality with a view to identifying a final solution (*Conclusion*). Drawing on additional sources—both online and print—they evaluate the reliability and validity of the chatbot's output and reflect on any limitations in their original instructions. In a final plenary session, the class compares and discusses their experience, while the teacher directs attention in particular to the user's role in interacting with the chatbot and to the broader issue of the reliability of online information, which affects humans and non-humans alike (*Discussion*).

This activity is suitable for secondary students but, with adaptation, can also be carried out in the later years of primary education. With younger pupils, it is advisable to adopt techniques such as *think-aloud* (Coiro, 2011) provide closer scaffolding: the teacher models interaction by verbalising prompts and responses, guiding pupils towards the discovery of unexpected behaviours.

2.2 *Problem-Solving as a Teaching Strategy to Promote Informed Attitudes Towards AI*

If in the previous section we dealt with critically contextualising user-side AI applications—thus emphasising the importance of becoming expert prompters—in this section we focus on critically contextualising machine-side AI applications; that is, looking inside them to grasp their grammar of operation under the rubric of explainability, with specific reference to ML applications.

From this point of view, problem-based learning appears to be a promising teaching approach by virtue of the variety of interpretations associated with the concept of problem-solving, ranging from narrower to broader meanings. In particular, problem-solving has long been an educational practice for the development of logical-mathematical skills. At the same time, from Dewey (1938) onwards, it has assumed the character of a broader style of inquiry and discovery, traceable to the concept of insight or *learning by discovery* (Bruner, 1961).

Proponents of problem-solving understood in this more general sense emphasise that engaging learners in the typical processes of researchers (hypothesis-testing) is the most stimulating way to increase motivation. As we shall see, in both cases (narrow meaning and logical-mathematical learning; broader meaning and learning by discovery), problem-solving can help to elucidate significant aspects of AI functioning.

The broader or narrower meaning of the concept of problem-solving is related to the very nature of the problem to be solved. In his work on the subject, Jonassen (2004) distinguished different types of problems in relation to four aspects:

1. **Structuredness**: Problems can be well-defined or ill-defined. The former requires the application of a finite and known number of concepts, rules, and principles in a domain where the solutions are already clear (e.g., arithmetic problems); the latter have unknown aspects, and the solution is unpredictable since there may be multiple acceptable outcomes (e.g., making a plan, defining an intervention strategy).
2. **Complexity**: The complexity of a problem is determined by the number of factors or variables involved, the type of relationships between them subsisting, and the degree of stability of these relationships over time; ill-defined problems tend to be more complex.
3. **Dynamicity**: Complex problems are usually dynamic, in the sense that the environment within which the task/problem is situated tends to change over time and it becomes necessary continually to seek new solutions.
4. **Domain (Context) specificity/abstractness:** Problem-solving tasks are situated and thus dependent on the nature of the context and cognitive domain.

In his taxonomy, considering the four variables described above, Jonassen (2004) identified eleven types of problems that can give rise to an equal number of teaching activities, fostering different cognitive strategies. They range from more well-defined problems such as the logic problem, algorithm, or rules application to less defined problems such as case analysis, design tasks, or dilemmas.

Typically, poorly or ill-defined problems form the basis of Problem-Based Learning (PBL), an instructional technique that confronts students with real-world, often complex and multidisciplinary problems, stimulating them to find solutions through research, collaboration, and critical application of acquired knowledge.

One of the main benefits of PBL with reference to AI is that it can position AI both as a problem to be explored and as a tool for finding solutions. For example, students might be asked to examine the implications of a facial-recognition system: in this scenario, AI and its decision-making mechanisms become the "problem." At the same time, they could use AI models to analyse large datasets or simulate complex scenarios, making it a "tool" for solving other problems.

PBL encourages students to formulate questions and hypotheses, and to test solutions, favouring critical inquiry and preparing them to make decisions in an uncertain world (Savery and Duffy, 1995). When applied to AI teaching (see subsequent teaching suggestions), this may involve exploring the limitations of an algorithm, identifying potential biases in the data, or considering the social implications of a specific technological application. Such inquiry helps students look beyond the surface of the technology, promoting deep and critical understanding.

Another pillar of PBL is its collaborative dimension. Students often work in groups—discussing, debating, and building solutions together. This collaboration can be especially fruitful in the field of AI, as learners with different skills and perspectives can offer unique insights.

Although the specific steps may vary slightly depending on the literature taken as reference, the basic phases typical of PBL are:

1. **Problem presentation.** It is posed not as a simple question with a clear answer, but as a complex problem—often lacking an unambiguous solution—that serves as a starting point and stimulus for learning.
2. **Problem analysis.** Once introduced, students work together to define the nature of the problem, identifying what they already know and what they need to find out in order to address it
3. **Research and investigation**. After outlining the problem, students undertake inquiry: consulting books, conducting online research, performing experiments, or carrying out interviews to acquire the knowledge and skills needed.
4. **Ideation and brainstorming.** Having gathered information, students generate a variety of possible solutions, promoting creativity and critical thinking.
5. **Solution development**. From the range of possibilities, students select and elaborate the approach or ideas they find most promising.

6. **Solution presentation**. Next, students present their solutions in forms that may include oral reports, written documents, prototypes, or simulations.
7. **Evaluation and reflection.** Students, together with the teacher, reflect both on the proposed solutions and on the learning process as a whole. This reflective stage is essential for consolidating learning and developing greater awareness of their own cognitive processes.
8. **Feedback**. Finally, the PBL cycle concludes with feedback from the teacher and peers, helping students understand how to refine their problem-solving skills.

Below we offer, as examples, two teaching proposals that leverage poorly or ill-defined PBL-style problems to foster a critical, problem-based approach to the topic of AI. The proposals are suitable for students in the second cycle of education; by simplifying the number of variables involved, both can also be applied in the later years of elementary schooling.

Problem No. 1—Exploring Decision-Making Mechanisms

- **Problem presentation**: A case in which a model produced an unexpected or incorrect result (e.g., during a classification or prediction task) is presented to students, without providing details of the underlying causes.
- **Example**: 10 August, a well-known weather service predicted snowfall in Rome during a period of warm, sunny days. How could an AI make such a serious mistake in forecasting the weather?
- **Problem definition**: Students gather in groups to discuss and better define what the underlying cause might be. What do they already know? What are their initial hypotheses?
- **Discussion example**: Is it possible that the model did not have access to the right data? Was there an unexpected climate variation?
- **Research and investigation**: Students attempt to understand how the model works, what kind of data were used, what might have caused the errors.
- **Example**: What other predictions has the model made in the past? Is this a recurrent error or a rarity?

- **Ideation and brainstorming**: Each group reflects on and discusses possible reasons for the error. Students could generate many hypotheses, from the most obvious to the most complex.
- **Example hypothesis** : The model may have relied on too little data sampling; there may have been a technical problem in data collection.
- **Solution development**: After discussion, each group selects one or two of the most promising hypotheses and develops a solution or a way to test them.
- **Example solution**: To test the data-sampling hypothesis, we could examine other predictions made by the same model under similar conditions and see whether the error recurs.
- **Solution presentation**: Each group presents its findings and investigative process.
- **Evaluation and reflection**: The class, together with the teacher, discusses the different solutions and reflects on what has been learned about the possible causes of the error and the importance of data literacy and explainability.
- **Feedback**: The instructor and other students give feedback on the various approaches and proposed solutions.

Problem No. 2—Building a Decision Tree

- **Problem identification**: Students are introduced to a problem requiring them to develop a decision-making system based on specific criteria.
- **Example**: A new restaurant hires a team of experts to build a decision-making model that can identify the "best pasta dish" to suggest based on customers' characteristics.
- **Problem definition**: Students, divided into groups, define the criteria the model will be used to make a decision.
- **Example**: Cooking time of the pasta; type of seasoning; age of the customer; time available; food allergies, etc.
- **Generation of alternative solutions**: Students consider different ways the identified criteria can be combined.
- **Example**: One team might propose that the customer's age should be the first criterion, assuming that older people prefer traditional dishes while younger people are open to experimentation. Another

team might start with the time available, assuming that those with less time will prefer dishes with shorter cooking times.

- **Evaluation and selection**: Students evaluate the various decision trees they have created, considering which might be most effective or accurate and discussing the advantages and disadvantages.
- **Example**: Each group drafts its own decision tree. Suppose a team proposes the following tree:
  - First node: How much time does the customer have? (< 30 minutes / > 30 minutes)
    If < 30 minutes, suggest dishes with short cooking time.
    If > 30 minutes, move on to the next node.
  - Second node: What is the customer's age? (young / elderly)
    If young, suggest innovative dishes.
    If elderly, suggest traditional dishes.
- **Implementation**: Students test their decision trees with various scenarios to see how they function in practice.
- **Example**: A 25-year-old customer with only 20 minutes to eat arrives at the restaurant. What is your suggestion? Groups use their tree to determine the recommended pasta dish.
- **Review and Evaluation**: Students reflect on the performance of their decision trees and consider possible modifications to improve them.
- **Example**: After testing scenarios, students may find that some criteria are not as decisive as expected. They may decide to give more weight to personal tastes or food allergies and adjust the tree accordingly.

References

ACRL (2016), *Framework for Information Literacy for Higher Education*, American Library Association, Chicago, IL (https://libguides.bentley.edu/informationliteracy/standards/framework).

Adadi A., Berrada M. (2018), *Peeking inside the black box: a survey on Explainability for machine learning*, in The Knowledge Engineering Review, pp. 52138–60.

AI HLEG (High-Level Expert Group on Artificial Intelligence) (2019), *Ethics Guidelines for Trustworthy AI*, European Commission, Brussels.

Arrieta A.B. *et al.* (2020), *Explainable Artificial Intelligence (XAI): Concepts, taxonomies, opportunities and challenges toward responsible AI*, in Information Fusion, 58, pp. 82–115.

Bhargava R., D'Ignazio C. (2015), *Designing tools and activities for data literacy learners*, in Workshop on Data Literacy, Webscience.

Borgman C. L. (2016), *Big Data, Little Data, No Data: Scholarship in the Networked World*, The MIT Press, Cambridge, MA.

Bruner J. S. (1961), *The Act of Discovery*, in Harvard Educational Review, 31, pp. 21–32.

Carmi E. *et al.* (2020), *Data citizenship: Rethinking data literacy in the age of disinformation, misinformation, and malinformation*, in Internet Policy Review, 9(2), pp. 1–22.

Chatterjee J., Dethlefs, N. (2023), *This new conversational AI model can be your friend, philosopher, and guide ... and even your worst enemy*, in Patterns, 4(1), 100676.

Coiro J. (2011), *Talking About Reading as Thinking: Modeling the Hidden Complexities of Online Reading Comprehension*, in "Theory into Practice," 50(2), pp. 107–15.

Dewey J. (1938), *Experience and Education*, Kappa Delta Pi, New York, NY.

Doshi-Velez F., Kim, B. (2017), *Towards A Rigorous Science of Interpretable Machine learning*, arXiv preprint arXiv:1702.08608, 2017.

Feldman-Maggor, Y., Cukurova, M., Kent, C., & Alexandron, G. (2025). *The impact of explainable AI on teachers' trust and acceptance of AI EdTech recommendations: The power of domain-specific explanations.* **International Journal of Artificial Intelligence in Education**. Advance online publication. https://doi.org/10.1007/s40593-025-00486-6

Ferraris, M. (2003). Navigare nel WWW a scuola: ma per andare dove?. Italian Journal of Educational Technology, 11(1), 29–29.

Freire P. (1970), *Pedagogia do Oprimido*, Paz e Terra, Rio de Janeiro.

García-Peñalvo, F. J. (2023), *The perception of artificial intelligence in educational contexts after the launch of ChatGPT: Disruption or panic?* in Education in the Knowledge Society, 24, e31279.

Ghodoosi, B., West, T., Li, Q., Torrisi-Steele, G., & Dey, S. (2023). *A systematic literature review of data literacy education.* Journal of Business & Finance Librarianship, 28(2), 112–127.

Jonassen D.H. (2004), *Learning to Solve Problems: An Instructional Design Guide*, Jossey-Bass, San Francisco (CA).

Lo, D. (2023, May). Trustworthy and synergistic artificial intelligence for software engineering: Vision and roadmaps. In *2023 IEEE/ACM International Conference on Software Engineering: Future of Software Engineering (ICSE-FoSE)* (pp. 69–85). IEEE.

Lundberg S. M., Lee S. I. (2017), *A unified approach to interpreting model predictions*, in Advances in Neural Information Processing Systems, 30, pp. 4765–74.

Nazaretsky, T., Mejia-Domenzain, P., Swamy, V., Frej, J., & Käser, T. (2025). *The critical role of trust in adopting AI-powered educational technology for learning: An instrument for measuring student perceptions*. Computers and Education: Artificial Intelligence, 8, 100368.

O'Neil C. (2016), *Weapons of Math Destruction: How Big Data Increases Inequality and Threatens Democracy*. Crown Publishing, New York, NY.

Pangrazio, L., & Selwyn, N. (2023). *Critical data literacies: rethinking data and everyday life*. MIT Press.

Pedaste M. *et al.* (2015), *Phases of inquiry-based learning: Definitions and the inquiry cycle*, in Educational research review, 14, pp. 47–61.

Perrotta C. *et al.* (2021), *Automation, APIs and the distributed labor of platform pedagogies in Google Classroom*, in "Critical Studies in Education," 62(1), pp. 97–113.

Poell T., Nieborg D., Van Dijck J. (2019), *Platformisation*, in Internet Policy Review, 8(4), pp. 1–13.

Ribeiro M.T., Singh S., Guestrin C. (2016), "*Why should I trust you?" Explaining the predictions of any classifier*, in *Proceedings of the 22nd ACM SIGKDD international conference on Knowledge Discovery and Data Mining*, (August 13–17, 2016, San Francisco, CA), Association for Computing Machinery, New York, NY, pp. 1135–44.

Savery J. R., Duffy T. M. (1995), *Problem based learning: An instructional model and its constructivist framework*, in "Educational technology," 35(5), pp. 31–8.

Schmarzo B. (2023), *AI & Data Literacy: Empowering Citizens of Data Science*, Packt Publishing, Birmingham.

Türkmen, G. (2025). The review of studies on explainable artificial intelligence in educational research. *Journal of Educational Computing Research*, *62*(4), 891–912. https://doi.org/10.1177/07356331241310915

Van Dijck, J. (2014), *Datafication, dataism and dataveillance: Big data between scientific paradigm and ideology*, in Surveillance and Society, 12(2), pp. 197–208.

Van Dijck, J., Poell, T., & De Waal, M. (2018). *The platform society: Public values in a connective world*. Oxford university press.

Wei, J., Wang, X., Schuurmans, D., Bosma, M., Xia, F., Chi, E., ... & Zhou, D. (2022). *Chain-of-thought prompting elicits reasoning in large language models*. Advances in Neural information processing systems, 35, 24824–24837.

The Ethical Dimension: General Principles and Educational Perspectives

Abstract This chapter addresses the ethical dimension of Artificial Intelligence Literacy, providing an overview of key principles and proposing pedagogical methods for their exploration. The first part reviews the main ethical challenges posed by AI, including issues of privacy, data bias, behavioural manipulation, and accountability. It synthesises a core set of guiding principles from prominent literature and policy documents—such as transparency, justice, non-maleficence, and responsibility. This chapter then re-contextualises these principles for the specific domain of education, incorporating child-centric considerations like pedagogical appropriateness, student rights, and teacher well-being. To translate these ethical concepts into classroom practice, the second part presents two dialogic teaching strategies. It recommends using structured Debate to engage students with controversial dilemmas and employing the case study method to ground abstract ethical principles in tangible, real-world scenarios. Ultimately, this chapter argues that fostering ethical deliberation through these methods is essential for developing the reflective and responsible judgement required to navigate an AI-driven society.

Keywords AI ethical challenges · AI ethical principles · AI · Pedagogy & children rights · Debating controversial topics · Analysing sensitive issues

M. Ranieri et al., *Artificial Intelligence in Schools*, Digital Education and Learning, https://doi.org/10.1007/978-3-032-15919-9_5

1 Themes and Issues

1.1 Ethics of Artificial Intelligence: Conceptual Foundations

How should we interpret the concept of accountability, and to whom should responsibility for actions, and their consequences, be attributed when decisions are made by or with the support of automated Artificial Intelligence (AI) systems? What are the risks and dangers related to discrimination and biases inherent in the use of AI technologies? How does the development of AI affect the privacy and security of personal data, and what ethical implications follow? What is the role of transparency in AI ethics, and to what extent can it help sustain trust in this technology?

These are some of the classic questions addressed by the field of AI ethics. This domain is not new: as Floridi (2023) notes, ethical debate on AI developed in the 1950s–1960s alongside the rise of AI as an academic discipline. However, interest in this area has intensified in recent times, owing to significant advances in the capabilities and applications of AI systems.

Müller (2020), in his introduction on the topic, situates AI ethics within applied ethics together with bioethics, environmental ethics, and so forth, while emphasising its dynamic and unstable character. Nevertheless, scholarship on the ethical aspects of AI is now extensive (Boddington, 2023; Machado and Silva, 2025; Stahl et al., 2023), as is the production of policy papers and recommendations (Floridi, 2023; Jobin et al., 2019; Sing, 2024).

The issues addressed in these works are diverse, and the underlying premises often differ. According to Floridi (2023), for instance, AI is not a new kind of intelligence but a new form of agency (see chapter "The Cognitive Dimension: Historical Framework and Basic Concepts"); the ethical challenges emerge from this unprecedented disjunction between action and intelligence, coupled with the technological "envelopment" of the world that AI engenders.

Müller (2020) provides a comprehensive review of the principal ethical issues surrounding AI that are currently debated in academic, political, and public arenas. In what follows, we draw on these issues as a conceptual basis for understanding the main ethical orientations that characterise contemporary reflection on the topic.

The first issue concerns privacy and surveillance. The increasing digitalisation of our lives has made the collection and storage of personal data and an ever more pervasive phenomenon—one that AI has greatly expanded, not least through novel forms of surveillance (Sinnreich and Gilbert, 2024). Captured data are exchanged among various actors, often for a fee. In this scenario, it is important to recognise that users exercise very little control over the process: data collection frequently occurs without adequate user awareness or through subtle forms of manipulation, and what appears to be free is actually not—hence the adage "services in exchange for data." Large technology companies base much of their business model on data collection, prompting some users to leave, while the majority appear to have lost the autonomy needed to break free from this control. Protecting personal data involves a multiplicity of legal challenges and is continually threatened by the difficulties lawmakers encounter in enforcing regulations.

The second issue pertains to behaviour manipulation, which AI systems can amplify through their ability to mine user data deeply and exploit individual vulnerabilities. Algorithms can target individuals or small groups through personalised stimuli designed to influence them, while the boundary between mere stimulus and outright manipulation is becoming increasingly blurred. Numerous organisations, especially in marketing and gambling, exploit behavioural biases, deception, and addiction generation to maximise profits making use of "dark patterns" (Müller, 2020) in interface design.

The third issue is the opacity of AI systems, a recurrent theme in ethical debates (Ross, 2022). Decision-automation technologies raise serious concerns regarding transparency, accountability, and the extent of human participation. Often, neither end users nor experts understand—nor can they explain—how a system arrives at its outcomes, rendering the process opaque and potentially amplifying the biases embedded in the data. As noted earlier (see chapter "The Critical Dimension: Understanding and Evaluation Beyond Automation"), many AI systems rely on machine learning methods that extract patterns from data; such patterns can be so opaque that even developers themselves are unable to explain or clarify how they were formed or to specify what data most strongly influenced the resulting decisions.

The fourth issue relates to bias in decision-making systems. Because such systems operate on data, their outputs can range from trivial recommendations, such as choosing a restaurant, to consequential judgements, such as a medical diagnosis or the granting of a loan. Among the frequently cited and most troubling cases is so-called predictive policing

(McDaniel and Pease, 2022), a rather disturbing concept that refers to the use of algorithmic forecasts to anticipate where and when law-enforcement resources will be needed. The central worry is the perpetuation (and amplification) of bias embedded in the historical data used to train these systems: feedback loops can trigger intensified policing in particular neighbourhoods and yield discriminatory outcomes for specific social groups. Detecting, measuring, and mitigating bias in AI systems remains a difficult challenge with far-from-obvious solutions.

The fifth issue in the AI-ethics debate focuses on human-robots interaction, a research area highly sensitive to the moral and social implications of human–machine encounters (Bartneck et al., 2021). AI-enabled robots could be used for improper purposes, including the manipulation of humans through behaviours that deceive or undermine human dignity. Additional concerns map onto familiar ethical-legal domains that apply to other technologies as well: product safety, liability, and prohibitions against deceptive advertising.

Further concerns relate to the impact of AI on work, the sixth issue highlighted by Müller (2020) in his review. AI and robotics promise substantial gains in productivity and wealth, yet automation is likely to reduce demand for human labour and to exacerbate labour-market polarisation—between highly specialised, service-or knowledge-intensive roles on one hand and, on the other, lower-mid-skill occupations that are readily automated (e.g., the supermarket cashier role increasingly displaced by self-checkout systems) (Filippi et al., 2023). In principle, the massive productivity dividends generated by automation could usher in an "age of leisure," but equitable wealth distribution remains a distant prospect.

By contrast, behind many AI systems lie armies of data labellers working in precarious conditions: low wages distributed through opaque subcontracting networks, compensation based on output that prioritises speed over accuracy, and minimal job security. Many operate in the Global South, handling large volumes of repetitive tasks or moderating disturbing images, or self-harm content without adequate psychological support. An additional challenge lies in addressing the implications for environmental sustainability. AI systems consume considerable energy—especially during ML training—and leave behind electronic waste that is difficult to recycle. In other words, while AI is often portrayed as an abstract and autonomous technological advancement, its development and functioning rely heavily on human labour—as we have noted—as well as on significant environmental resources. The physical infrastructures, energy consumption, and extractive practices required to support AI systems highlight the tangible costs of what is frequently described as a dematerialised process (Lindgren, 2023).

The seventh theme recurring in AI-ethics discussions centres on autonomous systems. To illustrate the issues more clearly, we turn to the example of autonomous vehicles (Krügel and Uhl, 2022). It is estimated that their use could significantly reduce the harm caused by human driving—ranging from fatalities and injuries in traffic accidents to certain forms of environmental pollution. Nevertheless, the ethical dilemmas remain numerous! Prominent among them are questions about balancing self-interest and the common good: regulatory frameworks tend to prioritise safety as the overriding goal, shifting responsibility away from individual drivers and towards manufacturers, technology providers, infrastructure operators, and policy and legal authorities. In short, the ethical landscape here resists simplification.

All this brings us directly to the heart of machine-ethics challenges, the next area flagged by Müller (2020). The term *machine ethics* refers to ethics for machines themselves—that is, treating machines as subjects, rather than merely addressing human use of machines as objects. For some authors, this idea rests on the premise that if machines act in ethically relevant ways, then a dedicated machine ethics is required. This position espouses a *strong* view: machine ethics should guarantee that a device's behaviour towards human users is ethically acceptable, beginning with basic issues such as product safety (Anderson and Anderson, 2007). Other scholars adopt a more circumscribed stance, arguing that machine ethics means designing AI systems capable of accounting for social values, moral and ethical considerations, and stakeholder priorities, while also explaining their reasoning to ensure transparency (Dignum, 2018).

Alongside the theoretical debate, recent years have also witnessed a proliferation of policy papers and guidelines on AI ethics. Floridi (2023) warns that the sheer volume of proposed ethical principles risks generating confusion and undesirable side effects—from ethical shopping (i.e., choosing whichever set of ethics best justifies one's behaviour) to ethical bluewashing (i.e., undertaking superficial actions merely to appear ethical) to ethical avoidance (i.e., ignoring the ethical issue altogether). Hence, it is crucial to identify a core of shared principles: a strategy that does not eliminate every problem but does help contain them.

Through a comparative analysis of some of the most robust ethical frameworks, Floridi (2023) outlined five core principles: (i) beneficence—AI should be developed for the common good of humanity and the sustainability of the planet; (ii) non-maleficence—AI must prevent misuse, such as privacy invasion or threats to security; (iii) autonomy—a balance must be struck between the decision-making power retained by humans and that delegated to machines; (iv) justice—AI development should promote fairness and strive to eliminate all forms of discrimination; and (v) explicability—encompassing both epistemic intelligibility (*How does it work?*) and ethical accountability (*Who is responsible for how it works?*).

Similarly, Jobin and colleagues (2019) sought to catalogue the ethical principles underpinning contemporary AI policies by analysing nearly one hundred documents including guidelines, frameworks, and recommendations. Their survey yielded eleven core principles, listed in order of prevalence: transparency; justice and equity; non-maleficence; accountability; privacy; beneficence; freedom and autonomy; trust; dignity; sustainability; and solidarity. Among these, the most frequently recurring are transparency, justice and fairness, non-maleficence, accountability, and privacy. Let us examine them more analytically, integrating the various perspectives.

Transparency. It is the principle most frequently mentioned. Transparency is indispensable, as we have noted, in contexts such as data collection and processing (*What is done with my personal information?*), or automated decision-making processes (*How are decisions about me reached?*), or personalised recommendation systems (*On what data is a particular product or news item shown to me?*). Transparency demands that answers to these questions be both accessible and comprehensible. The rationale is that transparent, explainable, or interpretable AI can minimise harm caused, improve human-AI interaction, increase trust in the technology, and uphold democratic values (Jobin et al., 2019). Another way to express the importance of transparency is to say that it empowers individuals with epistemic agency, i.e., the ability to understand what happens to their data and how AI uses them, as well as to exercise greater control over that information, thereby safeguarding personal autonomy. Central here is the notion of explainability. As we have seen, Floridi (2023) highlights its dual valence—epistemological and ethical—and argues that explainability undergirds the other principles, because only by understanding AI's actual benefits and risks can we decide whether, and to what extent, to delegate action to machines on our behalf. Traces of explainability as a regulatory principle appear also in various algorithmic directives: the concept of a right to explanation emerges, for instance, in the 2016 European Data Protection Regulation (Vredenburgh, 2022). Critics note, however, that we are still far from a fully realised right to explanation, and that its technical implementation remains unclear. Nevertheless, the right to explanation remains, in our view, a fundamental entitlement that—within today's algorithmic society—should be rightly counted among basic human rights (Tafani, 2023).

Justice, fairness, and solidarity. Justice is discussed in AI-ethics guidelines chiefly in relation to fairness on the one hand, and prejudice and discrimination on the other (Jobin et al., 2019). Equity concerns revolve around equal access to AI and the fair distribution of the technology's burdens and benefits (Selwyn, et al., 2023). For instance, the digital divide between nations that can afford to develop and deploy AI and those that lack access to state-of-the-art technologies is particularly troubling. The principle of non-discrimination is both fundamental and urgent: as noted earlier, algorithms or AI systems can embed biases by relying on non-inclusive datasets (*algorithmic bias*), thereby producing discriminatory outcomes and violating the ideal of fair and equitable AI. Less frequently cited, yet still significant, is the principle of solidarity, which addresses the just allocation of AI's benefits and harms (e.g., workers who lose their jobs owing to automation).

Non-maleficence and beneficence. Non-maleficence entails an active commitment to avoid harms arising from AI use. Such harms are typically framed as discrimination, privacy invasion, or physical injury; the principle is aimed above all at protecting individuals who are vulnerable to AI's effects. As AI adoption grows, people inevitably become subject to profiling and automated decision-making, their lives increasingly shaped by AI systems. It is therefore essential to ensure that AI does not harm citizens and, ideally, produces benefits that foster human empowerment (Waelen, 2022). Closely linked to no-harm policies is the requirement of robustness: an AI system should function correctly and reliably even when confronted with unexpected data, interference, or manipulation attempts. In other words, it must be built to manage uncertainty and withstand diverse forms of attack or anomaly.

Accountability, freedom, and autonomy. Accountability is often cited as a guiding principle for AI: the fear is that automated decisions may create accountability gaps (Gordon and Nyholm, 2021). AI systems can make decisions that directly affect humans, yet they cannot be held accountable—or called to account—for the consequences of their actions in the same way that humans can. This raises the question: who should (and can) be held responsible and accountable for harms caused by AI applications? This question brings us back to the issue of autonomy. According to Floridi (2023, p. 62), "[…] Humans should retain the power to decide which decisions to take and in what priority, exercising the freedom to choose where necessary and ceding it in cases were overriding reasons, such as efficacy, may outweigh the loss of control over decision- making. But any delegation should also remain overridable in principle, adopting an ultimate safeguard of deciding to decide again."

Privacy. Privacy can be viewed from several perspectives: as a value, a moral right, or a legal right. Jobin et al. (2019) observe that AI-ethics guidelines discuss privacy both as a value to be preserved and as a right to be protected. Moreover, privacy is often framed in relation to data protection, aligning with common definitions of privacy as "informational control" or "limited access" (DeCew, 2018). In both senses, privacy is understood as a dispositional power—specifically, the ability to control what happens to one's information and to determine who has access to it or other aspects of one's person. AI, therefore, is perceived as a potential threat to this ability because, as we have repeatedly pointed out in these pages, it entails the collection and analysis of vast quantities of personal data. AI could thus deprive individuals of their privacy power—or, put differently, privacy should be promoted precisely because it empowers data owners.

Trust. The need for trusted AI encompasses AI research, the organisations and people who develop it, design principles, and users' relationship with the technology (Jobin et al., 2019). Trust can be fostered by transparency or by ensuring that AI meets public expectations. The requirement to trust how AI is designed and developed can be interpreted as protection against the exercise of power by others. Trust is a desirable feature of the relationship between technology and its users: when one trusts or relies on an AI system, one expects that it will not abuse the power that such technology can exert over individuals in terms of control, manipulation, and conditioning. Therefore, in calling for trusted AI, we are asking that AI refrain from exercising power over us in an arbitrary, harmful, or excessive manner (Waelen, 2022).

Generally, guidelines and codes of ethics do not address topics such as machine ethics or the moral status of AI systems. Despite the diversity of positions, there is a broadly shared concern about the risks posed by machines' increasing capacity to act autonomously and by society's growing dependence on the technology itself.

1.2 Artificial Intelligence in Education: A Pedagogical Approach to Ethical Challenges

Developments in AI are also generating a wide range of intelligent tools and services in education, introducing various forms of automation into instructional systems (Perrotta et al., 2021; Peláez-Sánchez et al., 2024). As we saw in chapter "The Operational Dimension: Uses and Applications", these innovations span intelligent tutoring systems, automated-assessment devices, tools for personalising learning paths, and much more. Nevertheless, policy discourse has largely focused on adults, devoting limited attention to the impact of AI on children and adolescents (Irwin et al., 2021) and on education itself (Adams et al., 2023). In 2020 UNICEF reviewed twenty national AI strategies and found that most referred to children and their specific needs only in passing (Penagos et al., 2020). Even guidelines on AI ethics of AI in education remain scarce, although classroom-related ethical issues can be at least as critical as those confronting society at large (Luckin et al., 2022).

Within this climate of limited visibility, several recent initiatives suggest a shift: organisations such as UNICEF (2021), UNESCO (2021), and the European Union (Charisi et al., 2022) have called for AI-ethics principles to be interpreted in light of children's unique characteristics, rights, and educational contexts. Consequently, the ethical principles outlined in the previous section must be contextualised to safeguard the fundamental needs of children and adolescents and to meet the specific educational demands of this age group. In particular, as highlighted by Ranieri (2025), tensions between pedagogical imperatives and the automation of educational processes can give rise to genuine *aporiae* (A), with significant ethical implications, as shown below.

(A1) Automation vs Autonomy. Instructional AI operates as a decision-making system promising personalisation and optimisation, yet platformisation narrows learners' choices through opaque, proprietary algorithms. Such delegation risks attenuating the developmental work of exercising independent judgement and cultivating personal autonomy. Over time, learners may internalise the algorithm's preferences as their own, reducing opportunities for deliberation, experimentation, and productive failure.

(A2) Reproduction vs Creation. Generative systems primarily recombine learned statistical patterns, a process that risks displacing students' own inventive work and call into question the originality of AI-assisted outputs. Yet, when deliberately constrained and critically used, these systems can also expand the students' exploratory space, provoking ideas that learners must appropriate, transform, and refine—thereby supporting genuinely original creativity rather than replacing it.

(A3) Opacity vs Understanding. Black-box machine- and deep-learning models conflict with pedagogical imperatives of comprehensibility, an imperative underpinning all taxonomies of learning objectives, beginning with Bloom's (1956). After all, teachers cannot reasonably ask students to achieve understanding through mechanisms they themselves cannot understand. Without explainability, teachers and students cannot interrogate decisions or provide metacognitively rich feedback; educational AI must therefore offer interpretable rationales.

(A4) Mimesis vs Trust. Human-like outputs facilitate engagement but complicate academic integrity and evaluative trust. Undisclosed student reliance on AI or fully automated grading can erode confidence in authorship and assessment, generating anxiety and scepticism. Stated differently, the very realism which makes AI a persuasive tutor simultaneously obscures the boundary between authentic learner performance and algorithmic supplementation: teachers cannot readily distinguish genuine effort from AI-produced text, while students may doubt whether grades reflect their own competences or the model's capacities. Over time, this ambiguity can weaken the pedagogical contract, discouraging risk-taking and honest error—both prerequisites for deep learning.

(A5) Standardisation vs Personalisation. Although adaptive systems tailor pathways, they are trained on standardised datasets that may encode cultural bias. Putatively "individualised" experiences can thus homogenise learning and reproduce inequities unless educators actively counterbalance them. Over time, this can narrow curricular diversity, filtering out local languages, epistemologies, and marginal voices in favour of statistically dominant norms. Mitigation demands culturally responsive oversight—auditing training data, injecting locally sourced materials, and retaining teacher discretion—so that personalisation expands rather than constrains learners' horizons.

(A6) Speed vs Depth. Instantaneous AI responses accelerate access to information but may incentivise superficial consumption, displacing the slower, reflective processes required for deep learning and critical reasoning. Effective design treats AI output as a point of departure for verification, comparison, and argumentation rather than a terminal answer. Structured prompts that require students to interrogate sources, trace reasoning steps, or generate counterexamples can reintroduce productive delay, ensuring that speed becomes an entryway to inquiry rather than a substitute for it.

Addressing these *aporiae* demands pedagogical approaches that leverage AI's affordances while safeguarding autonomy, creativity, transparency, trust, diversity, and epistemic depth—approaches, in short, that are sensitive to the ethical requirements of AI. So, which ethical principles should be adopted within educational contexts?

In a recent paper, Adams and colleagues (2023) conducted a systematic analysis of several key documents on the subject (WEF, 2019; IEAIED, 2021; UNESCO, 2021; UNICEF, 2021; EC, DGEYSC, 2022). From this perspective, they reinterpreted the ethical principles systematised by Jobin et al. (2019), integrating them with more specifically pedagogical reflections. Below, we elaborate on the contribution of this rereading, complementing it with our own considerations aimed at connecting—when appropriate—each ethical principle to the corresponding aporia (A1–A6), together with further readings on the ethical dimensions of AI in education (Gouseti et al., 2024).

The principles of transparency, justice and equity, non-maleficence, accountability, privacy, beneficence, freedom, and autonomy appear across the various ethical-guidance documents, yet they are nuanced according to the target audience and educational context. In particular, with respect to **transparency**, we underscore the need to use language appropriate for children and adolescents so as to enhance the comprehensibility and explainability of AI (A3). As underlined above, understanding is imperative in education; it is a cornerstone of thinking itself. Learning to think in conditions of opacity becomes difficult. Moreover, formal educational processes culminate in assessments with certifying value. As adults responsible for the educational process, we must be able to explain why a given student performance has been evaluated positively or not: learners have a right to understand the basis of the grade—typically expressed numerically—that they receive. The importance of an explanation for the grade assigned spans both ethical and epistemic dimensions. Ethically, access to an explanation enables a *counter-explanation*, which—drawing on the same evidence—may yield different conclusions. Epistemically, an explanation helps identify the source of an error: on the metacognitive level, it fosters self-regulatory skills. In short, explainability and the right to explanation in education are crucial on multiple fronts. Introducing non-explainable systems into the management of classroom information and knowledge risks undermining the trust that underpin the educational relationship (A4).

Turning to **justice and equity**, educational systems must guarantee the inclusion of all children and adolescents (A6). The adoption of AI technologies should not exacerbate gaps between those who can access such tools and those who cannot; on the contrary, AI solutions ought to enhance equity and reduce social and digital exclusion of disadvantaged groups.

With regard to **privacy**, repeated emphasis is placed on the *right to be forgotten* as a safeguard for childhood and adolescence. Concerning **autonomy**, the guidelines highlight the need to obtain not only parental consent for the use of AI in the classroom but also the informed consent of the students themselves (A1).

To these principles, Adams and colleagues (2023) propose adding four others calibrated specifically to the school context and to the use of AI in education (AIED): pedagogical appropriateness; children's and adolescents' rights; AI literacy; and teacher well-being.

Pedagogical adequacy. The principle of pedagogical appropriateness directs teachers' attention to their educational responsibilities both to their discipline and to the care and well-being of children and adolescents. Accordingly, when adopting AI applications for teaching, educators must take into account what is good, right, and enriching for students in their specific school community, weighing whether—and to what extent—the benefits of AI use clearly outweigh the risks by facilitating particular learning tasks across different subjects (UNESCO, 2021). The importance of deploying AI through evidence-based school practices, while continuously monitoring and evaluating its effects, is emphasised (IEAIED, 2021). Concretely, pedagogical appropriateness can be assessed across a range of factors: the relevance of a curricular resource to a child's developmental stage; the readability or difficulty level of a text; and the congruence of an instructional technique or approach with the task at hand or the particular group of students involved. In every case, educational AI applications must be adapted to learners' developmental stages, tailoring technologies to the ways children and adolescents learn (A5, A6).

Equally notable are concerns about AI's potential impact on students' sense of efficacy and agency (A1). Highly adaptive AI could reduce peer interaction time, increase machine-made decisions, and shift emphasis towards knowledge that is easier to automate—thereby depriving students of opportunities to cultivate ingenuity, self-efficacy, and other critical twenty-first-century skills such as self-regulation, metacognition, critical thinking, creativity, and independent thought (UNESCO, 2021). Thus, pedagogical appropriateness also requires careful balancing against other AI-ethics principles, including freedom and autonomy. A similar balancing act is needed when AI is used for assessment (IEAIED, 2021). Integrating AI into educational platforms could facilitate a move from summative, product-focused assessment towards continuous assessment capable of monitoring multiple factors and capturing a broader spectrum of learning. The downside is that constant monitoring may leave students feeling exposed during lessons (A1, A5).

Pedagogical appropriateness likewise encompasses broader issues concerning child-welfare protection and policy guidance. UNICEF (2021) states that any educational AI application must be evaluated for risks and opportunities in the best interests of the child: while AI can enhance the delivery of educational services, it can also limit growth opportunities through predictive profiling, exclude or discriminate against certain children owing to algorithmic bias, and/or deepen the digital divide (A5). There is also discussion of "algorithms for children" (WEF, 2019, p. 7), highlighting how, on the one hand, they can guide learners towards positive educational goals and outcomes, while on the other they risk triggering problems of *algorithmic manipulation*. Rather, the goal should be to create enabling AI environments centred on the needs of children and adolescents, using participatory research carried out *for* and *with* them, as also emphasised from a European-Union perspective (EU, 2022). In this regard, several authors (Perrotta, 2022; Raffaghelli, 2023) argue for the construction of a genuine deontological framework that ensures the fair, just, and non-discriminatory use of data—*data justice*—in education, engaging the wider community in a public dialogue about the unfair impacts of algorithmic decisions.

Finally, when a technology is adopted, an almost intimate relationship arises between the individual and the device—so much so that technologies are sometimes described as extensions of the self. When AI becomes a *prosthesis* for a child or adolescent through classroom integration, teachers, educators, and administrators must reflect not only on its pedagogical effectiveness and learning outcomes but also on possible negative implications that could impair or diminish harmonious development in moral or social terms (Turkle, 2018), identity formation (Clark, 2018), or mental health and cognitive autonomy (Vold & Hernández-Orallo, 2021).

Rights of children and adolescents. Including children's rights among the ethical principles guiding AI applications in education means recognising a distinct set of rights that apply worldwide to children and adolescents. The 1989 United Nations Convention on the Rights of the Child affirms, among other protections, the right to a healthy, happy, and secure childhood free from discrimination; the right to a free and enriching education; and the right to privacy—all of which are fundamental when regulating AI use in educational settings. Subsequently, General Comment No. 25 (2021) extends the Convention's application to the digital environments, clarifying that children's rights must be fully guaranteed online through an integrated approach that reconciles potentially conflicting rights, such as those of protection and participation. In parallel, both UNICEF (2021) and WEF (2019) insist on the need to include the rights of children and adolescents in AI policies. Because of their specific vulnerabilities, children and adolescents require age-appropriate language and comprehension, attention to the malleability of values and ideas, safeguards against algorithmic manipulation and reduced autonomy, robust data- and privacy-protection (incidentally, questions arise over how much access parents should have to their children's data at different developmental stages, and for what purposes). Additional concerns include shielding young people from physical and psychological harm and preventing the misuse of tutor robots that could impede socio-emotional growth.

AI Literacy. The construct of AI literacy (AIL), which is the specific subject matter of this volume, is generally concerned with knowledge of basic AI concepts, skills needed to engage critically with AI applications, and awareness of the ethical considerations involved in creating and using AI (see chapter "The Dimensions of Artificial Intelligence Literacy: A Pedagogical Perspective"). Including AIL among the ethical principles governing educational AI, especially in primary and secondary schools, signals the importance that international bodies attach to educating younger learners about these issues. UNESCO (2021, p. 23) explicitly envisions "a pedagogy that, rather than focusing on what computers are good at (e.g. memorizing and computation), puts more emphasis on human skills (e.g. critical thinking, communication, collaboration and creativity) and the ability to collaborate with pervasive AI tools in life, learning, and work." Implementing such a pedagogy naturally demands AI literacy not only for students but also for teachers and parents (Akgun and Greenhow, 2021).

Teacher well-being. Teachers' well-being is a multifaceted concept encompassing physical, psychological, and mental health, as well as the ability to manage personal resources in a balanced, dynamic manner amid the many challenges of the school environment. In the specific case of AI integration into school practices, teacher well-being must be considered in relation to a plurality of aspects such as increased workload, the need for continuous professional development, additional time for instructional preparation, possible reduction in meaningful teacher-student relationships, and the spectre of technological unemployment. Because teachers' well-being is closely linked to students' well-being, educators need adequate time and space to learn about emerging technological scenarios and to familiarise themselves with current debates on AI and its ethical implications.

Following this discussion, it is worth noting that the ethical-pedagogical principles formulated by various international bodies share an assumption that Adams and colleagues (2023) describe as the humanistic or anthropocentric bias. In brief, an anthropocentric perspective regards humans as autonomous agents, separate from—and superior to—all other entities, including technologies. Against this view, these authors juxtapose posthumanism, a line of inquiry that recognises the shifting hybrids and intersections between humans and machines, where the boundaries between human and non-human are increasingly blurred (Braidotti, 2013; Haraway, 2013). Humans interacting with AI thus become *human–AI* or *AI–human* hybrids, embedded in heterogeneous relationships. Overcoming an anthropocentric outlook carries clear ethical and normative consequences. Fabris (2019) observes that anthropocentric self-referentiality—common in debates on AI's societal role—fails to take the activity of machines adequately into account, regulating them with laws that can be easily circumvented. As an alternative, he proposes "the explicit adoption of a relational conception of human beings" (ivi, p. 106), which yields two advantages: first, it avoids framing the human-machine relationship solely in terms of subordination and control; second, it enables us "explicitly to pose the problem of what these entities can do, and to judge and evaluate that activity according to ethical parameters" (ibid.). This approach distinguishes "the action proper to human beings, in the multiplicity of its articulations and specific structure, from that - programmed and procedural, albeit 'adaptable' to its environment and capable of unprecedented developments - which is proper to the machine" (ibid.).

The pedagogical implication of this vision, in our view, lies in seeking conditions for collaboration among teachers, students, and machines, whereby the educational process for which humans are co-responsible finds in the machine a didactic ally that can enhance critical thinking, dialogic development, and creativity. Translating this vision into practice is not straightforward, however, given the substantial social, political, and economic asymmetry between technology users and technology producers. Nonetheless, schools and the wider educational sector cannot remain on the sidelines of discussions about the rights and duties of the parties in this complex web of relationships.

Critical AI literacy and, specifically, the educational activities that follow—aim to equip users, especially students who are future citizens, with the ability to make their voices heard on issues that directly affect them, without shortcuts and with full awareness of the surrounding complexity.

2 Methods and Tools

2.1 Debate as a Teaching Tool for Exploring Ethical Dilemmas in AI

When addressing ethical issues in school, one certainly cannot rely on directive, unidirectional teaching methods. Ethics concerns values, and values reflect different conceptions of good and evil. In other words, ethical issues represent inherently controversial content, and teaching on controversial topics requires pedagogical-didactic stances that are authentically open to dialogue, confrontation, and argumentation (Hobbs, 2021).

Thus, discussing in school the ethical challenges of AI—and the ethical dilemmas its development raises—entails the teacher's adopting a different posture towards students, one capable of acknowledging and accepting the diversity that stems from irreducible positions and from the uncertainty that arises when no single answer suffices. This holds in many fields, but it is especially true in an area as contentious as AI ethics.

A useful teaching technique for exploring AI-related ethical dilemmas, without falling into the fallacy of turning values to be debated into facts to be transmitted, is the debate format. This technique involves a structured confrontation between two individuals or teams defending opposing theses. Each side first argues in favour of its own position (Pro), then against the opposing one (Con), with the possibility of mutual rebuttals.

Within the school setting, debate offers teachers and students the chance to activate cognitive and metacognitive processes: in fact, the aim is not so much to win as to improve argumentative skills and deepen critical understanding (Dickson et al., 2015).

Typically, a debate unfolds through these phases: identification of the topic; division of the class into working groups; a workshop phase for gathering data and information to support each side's arguments; the in-class debate itself, with presentation of the pro and con cases, and their supporting evidence; and a final phase of synthesis and evaluation. The latter can be carried out by the teacher or by a group of students, using grids or rubrics. Speaking times are predefined and limited to a few minutes; therefore, each student must be able to communicate their viewpoint within the allotted time.

The benefits of debate extend to both the cognitive sphere, encompassing study strategies, oral expression, written production, critical thinking, and argumentative skills, and the relational sphere, because debate teaches participants to collaborate in groups, defend their opinions, regulate their emotions, and engage or persuade an audience. The effectiveness of this technique is well documented. Osborne (2005), for example, found that classroom debate fosters the acquisition of disciplinary knowledge while providing opportunities to demonstrate critical reading and writing skills. Dickson (2004) likewise argues that debate promotes writing proficiency, teamwork, analytical ability, and critical thinking. Moreover, debate enables teachers to create a learning environment that encourages knowledge construction through active participation.

How to implement a debate on AI ethical challenges at school? Conducting an educational activity on AI ethics first requires laying a foundation of background knowledge. The content provided in the previous chapters, particularly in chapter "The Cognitive Dimension: Historical Framework and Basic Concepts", serves as essential groundwork for an informed and productive discussion. Debate topics can be multifaceted. The following are illustrative proposals for activities conceived for students aged 14 and above, which can nonetheless be adjusted to suit different developmental stages and school environments.

Dilemma No. 1—Privacy and Personal-Data Protection

The Situation

Schools today often use AI-powered learning platforms that adapt lessons to each student's progress. These systems collect a lot of information: how fast students answer questions, what they get right or wrong, and how they behave when studying. This can make learning more personalised and efficient, helping teachers spot learning difficulties early. However, the same data can reveal personal and private details about students. What happens to that data? Who owns it—the student, the school, or the company that makes the software? Could it be used for something other than learning?

The Big Question

Does collecting and analysing student data through AI learning systems invade students' privacy, or does it help improve learning by personalising education and supporting teachers?

Questions to Think About

- Should schools be allowed to track how students learn?
- What kind of information is too personal to collect?
- Is it fair to be monitored in class by technology?
- Can we have both privacy and personalised learning at the same time?
- How should students be involved in decisions about their own data?

Cross-Curricular Connections

- ICT: understand how AI systems work, data use, and online safety.
- Civic Education/Philosophy: discuss digital rights, privacy laws, and responsible citizenship.
- Language & Communication: practice debate and persuasive writing about technology.
- Science: explore how data and innovation affect society and ethics.
- Economics: examine how companies profit from data and balance innovation with protection.
- Art & Media: create visuals on AI's pros and cons and analyse media portrayals of technology.

Debate Activity

Divide the class into two groups:

- **Pro-AI**: AI helps students learn better.
- **Privacy First**: AI threatens students' rights.

Each group research arguments connected to the big question from different subject perspectives.

A third group acts as a jury, evaluating arguments based on evidence, logic, and ethical reasoning.

Conclude with a joint class discussion on how to make technology in education both useful and fair.

Eventually, extend the task by asking students to co-create a "Student Privacy and Learning Charter," summarising key principles for using AI safely and ethically in schools—combining what they have learned from all the subjects.

Dilemma No. 2—Inequality and Equity

The Situation

Artificial Intelligence is changing the way students learn all over the world. Online lessons, virtual tutors, and AI-based educational platforms can make learning more flexible and accessible. For example, students in small towns or remote areas can now attend classes online, use digital resources, and even learn languages or coding through smart applications.

But not everyone has the same access to technology. Some students have fast internet, new devices, and digital skills, while others may struggle with poor connections, old computers, or limited support at home. If AI-based learning depends on these resources, could it make inequalities worse, leaving behind those who already face challenges?

The Big Question

Can AI in education increase inequality, favouring students from certain socio-economic or cultural backgrounds, or can it reduce barriers to learning by offering opportunities to students who might otherwise be excluded?

Questions to Think About

- Does everyone have equal access to the digital tools needed for AI-based learning?
- Can AI really replace traditional teaching for all types of learners?
- How might economic, cultural, or language differences affect students' experience with technology?
- Should governments and schools ensure equal digital access for every student?

- How can AI be used to include, not exclude, those who are disadvantaged?

Cross-Curricular Connections

- ICT: explore how AI and digital tools shape learning and reduce the digital divide.
- Civic Education/Philosophy: debate equity, fairness, and inclusive education linked to UN SDG 4.
- Language & Communication: practise debate and writing on AI's role in fair education.
- Science & Technology: discuss ethical AI design and data bias.
- Economics & Social Studies: examine how resources and access affect global education.
- Art & Media: create and analyse media showing AI's promise and risks for inclusion.

Debate Activity

Divide the class into two groups:

- **AI reduces inequality**: it brings learning to everyone, everywhere.
- **AI increases inequality**: it benefits only those who already have advantages.

Each group researches examples and evidence from different subject perspectives.

A jury team evaluates which side presents stronger, fairer, and more inclusive solutions.

Conclude with a class reflection: How can technology help build a fairer education system?

Eventually, extend the task by asking students to work in small groups to design a short "Digital equity plan for our school"—a set of practical actions to make learning with technology fair and accessible to all students.

Dilemma No. 3—Bias and Discrimination the Situation

The Situation

Artificial Intelligence (AI) is increasingly being used in education—for example, to grade tests, recommend learning materials, or evaluate students' performance. These systems are trained using large amounts of data collected from real people and past situations. But what if the data itself contains biases or stereotypes? If AI learns from examples that reflect unfair treatment or discrimination—for instance, favouring certain languages, genders, or cultural backgrounds—it might repeat or even amplify those biases. This means that some students could receive unfair assessments or fewer opportunities just because of who they are. At the same time, some argue that AI could actually reduce human bias by making decisions based on objective criteria rather than emotions or personal opinions.

It could even be used to detect hidden discrimination in textbooks, exams, or teaching practices.

The Big Question

Might AI inherit and reproduce human biases, leading to unfair treatment of some students, or can it reduce discrimination by offering objective, data-based assessments and helping uncover bias in education?

Questions to Think About

- Can technology ever be truly neutral and fair?
- If AI is trained on biased data, who is responsible for the results—the machine or the humans who built it?
- Could AI ever understand human diversity and cultural differences?
- How might bias in AI affect students' grades, opportunities, or confidence?
- Could AI be part of the solution—for example, by spotting biased language in textbooks or exams?

Cross-Curricular Connections

- ICT: learn how AI is trained, how bias arises, and how to design fair algorithms.

- Civic Education/Philosophy: discuss justice, equality, and responsibility in ethical AI use.
- Language & Communication: examine biased language and debate whether technology can be objective.
- Science & Technology: explore how data and algorithms mirror human choices and limitations.
- Economics & Social Studies: analyse how AI bias impacts jobs, education, and inequality.
- Art & Media: study stereotypes in media and create campaigns promoting fairness in AI.

Debate Activity

Divide the class into two groups:

- **AI as a fair tool**: AI reduces human bias by applying consistent, objective rules.
- **AI as a biased system**: AI repeats and strengthens existing human prejudices.

Each group gathers examples, evidence, and ethical arguments from different school subjects.

A jury team evaluates arguments based on fairness, use of evidence, and creativity.

Conclude with a reflection discussion: How can we make AI fairer and more inclusive in schools?

Eventually, extend the task by asking students to work together to draft a "Fair AI in Education Manifesto"—a set of principles ensuring that AI supports equality, diversity, and justice in learning environments.

Dilemma No. 4—Employment and Efficiency in the Age of Artificial Intelligence

The Situation

Artificial Intelligence (AI) is rapidly transforming the way people work, produce, and live.

Machines and computer programs can now perform many tasks once done only by humans—from assembling products and managing warehouses to writing texts or analysing data.

Supporters of AI argue that this technology can make life easier and more efficient. It can take over boring or dangerous jobs, reduce errors, and give people more time for creative or meaningful activities. For example, AI systems can help doctors diagnose diseases faster, or help teachers manage large groups of students more effectively.

However, others worry that the rise of AI could cause massive job losses, especially in sectors like manufacturing, transport, and even services.

If machines become cheaper and more efficient than people, will there still be enough work for everyone? And if so, will the new jobs created by AI be available to all—or only to those with advanced technical skills?

The big question

Can AI improve our lives by making them more efficient and productive, or will it worsen them by replacing human workers and increasing unemployment?

Questions to think about

- Which jobs are most at risk of being replaced by AI?
- Could AI create new types of jobs that we can't even imagine yet?
- How should society help people who lose their jobs because of automation?
- Is efficiency always a good thing, or can it have human costs?
- Should there be limits or regulations on how companies use AI in the workplace?

Cross-Curricular Connections

- ICT: explore how AI and robotics transform industries and create new careers.
- Civic Education/Philosophy: debate fair employment, ethics, and lifelong learning in an AI economy.
- Language & Communication: practice debate and writing on AI as a threat or opportunity.

- Science & Technology: study machine learning, automation benefits, and ethical design.
- Economics & Social Studies: examine how AI reshapes jobs, income, and productivity.
- Art & Media: analyse how culture imagines the future of work and human creativity.

Debate Activity

Divide the class into two groups:

- **Pro-AI side**: AI makes our lives better by improving efficiency and creating new opportunities.
- **Anti-AI side**: AI threatens jobs and risks increasing inequality.

Each group gathers examples from real life and different subject areas.

A jury group evaluates which team presents the most convincing and balanced arguments.

Conclude with a whole-class reflection: What kind of future do we want—and what role should humans play in it?

Eventually, extend the task by asking students to design a short "Future of Work Charter" outlining how technology, education, and ethics should work together to ensure that AI serves people—not the other way around.

Dilemma No. 6—AI and the Environment Impact

The Situation

Artificial Intelligence can have a major impact on the environment—both positive and negative.

On one hand, AI can help protect the planet by improving energy efficiency, predicting climate change, reducing waste, and supporting scientists in developing sustainable solutions. For example, AI can optimise energy use in cities, predict natural disasters, monitor deforestation, or analyse climate data to design better strategies against global warming.

On the other hand, AI systems consume enormous amounts of energy. The large data centres that power AI require electricity and cooling, producing greenhouse gas emissions. In addition, the production and disposal of electronic devices contribute to pollution and electronic waste (e-waste).

So, is AI really helping the environment—or harming it?

The Big Question

Does Artificial Intelligence help or harm the environment? Can it truly reduce pollution and fight climate change, or does it consume energy and cause environmental damage?

Questions to Think About

- In what ways can AI help protect the environment and reduce human impact on the planet?
- How much pollution does the technology behind AI systems generate?
- Is it possible to develop a "green" or sustainable AI?
- Who is responsible for making technologies more environmentally friendly—companies, governments, or users?
- How can we use technology in a conscious and sustainable way?

Cross-Curricular Connections

- Science & Environmental Education: explore how AI supports sustainability and the impact of tech production on the planet.
- ICT: study energy use in data centres and examples of Green AI.
- Civic Education/Philosophy: discuss citizens' and institutions' environmental responsibilities in the digital age.
- Language & Communication: debate and write about AI's role in protecting—or harming—the environment.
- Economics & Social Studies: examine how innovation, growth, and sustainability interact globally.
- Art & Media: create and analyse media promoting eco-friendly and sustainable technology.

Debate Activity

Divide the class into two groups:

- **AI helps the environment**: AI is a valuable tool for sustainability and fighting climate change.
- **AI harms the environment**: AI increases energy consumption and pollution.

Each group prepares examples and arguments from different subject perspectives.

A jury group evaluates which side presents the most convincing and balanced arguments.

Conclude with a class discussion on how to balance technological progress with environmental protection.

Eventually, extend the task by asking students to work in small groups to create a "Green Tech Plan for Our School"—a list of concrete actions to reduce the environmental impact of technology (responsible device use, recycling, saving energy, raising awareness).

2.2 *The Case Study as a Teaching Tool for Analysing AI Ethical Aspects*

Next to debate, another teaching technique well suited to sensitive and controversial topics—such as the ethical issues surrounding AI use and development—is the case study. Originally employed in legal education, this method has since been adopted in a range of disciplines, including medicine, economics, engineering, agriculture, receiving particular attention within constructivist circles (see for example Kinzie et al., 1998 or more recently Bonney, 2015), especially for its capacity to foster critical-thinking skills (Popil, 2011).

In a case-study approach, students are presented with a real or plausible problem or scenario that they must analyse, hypothesise about, or resolve by making the most appropriate decisions in light of the circumstances provided. Reynolds (1980) classified cases into three basic types:

1. **Decision-oriented case study** (*decision* or dilemma *cases*): Students are shown the problems that the protagonist(s) of a narrative

must face or the decisions they must make. The case is described with emphasis on the problem to be solved and introducing the decision-maker(s) at the moment of crisis. It can be enriched with informational materials that provide insight into the overall context, as well as supplementary resources such as tables, charts, letters, or documents on which can draw when formulating possible solutions.

2. **Problem identification and analysis case study** (*appraisal* or *issue cases*): Participants receive material, and the instructor poses straightforward questions such as "*What happened - or what is happening - here?*." Typically, there is no protagonist, and students are not asked to make a decision; instead, they analyse and evaluate the issues raised by the case.
3. **Case histories**: These are completed narratives and are generally less engaging than the previous types precisely because they have already reached a conclusion. They can serve as illustrative models to be emulated—for example, recounting a scientific discovery to help students understand how such breakthroughs occur.

Regardless of type, the purpose of the case-study method is not to find a single "right" solution, but to present plausible scenarios that prompt students to reflect by analysing real-world situations. For this reason, the method is well suited to educational proposals in applied ethics, including AI ethics. One major drawback is the rapid obsolescence of case studies, especially in technology: a case may remain relevant for only two or three years before it requires updating.

With classroom implementation in mind, we propose below two potential dilemma cases, to be adapted to the students' grade level and supplemented with contextualised informational materials. The teacher introduces each case and its guiding question. Working in groups, students review the provided documentation and discuss the possible courses of action under the given circumstances. At the end of the activity, groups share their conclusions with the class. Using an appropriate rubric, groups can evaluate one another, assessing the quality of each argument and the effectiveness of the proposed solution.

Case Study No.1—Creativity vs Automation: Can AI-Generated Art Be "Authentic"?

Context

In recent years, Artificial Intelligence has begun creating poems, paintings, songs, and even films. With tools like DALL·E, Midjourney, and ChatGPT, anyone can type a few words and instantly produce artworks that look like they were made by professional artists. But this raises an important question: Can art made by machines truly be called "authentic" or "creative"?

The Story

Ana, a 17-year-old high school student, has always loved art. She spends hours sketching portraits, experimenting with colours, and expressing her emotions through painting. One day, her school announces an art contest titled "The Future of Creativity." The rules are simple: students can submit any visual artwork representing how they imagine creativity will evolve in the future.

Ana plans to create a painting by hand, but her friend John shows her an AI image generator. "Look," he says, typing a few words into the app: "a futuristic city painted in the style of Van Gogh." In seconds, the AI produces a dazzling, colourful image. Ana is amazed—it's stunning, maybe even better than what she could paint herself. John enters his AI-generated artwork in the contest. Others in their class start doing the same.

Now Ana faces a dilemma. Should she:

- submit her own handmade painting, which reflects her emotions, thoughts, and hard work—but may not look as "perfect" as the AI images?
- use the AI tool to create something more visually impressive, even though she didn't physically make it herself?

The contest rules don't forbid AI-generated art, but the jury emphasises "originality and creativity." Ana wonders: If an algorithm makes the image, is it still creative? And if she prompts the AI—choosing the words and ideas—does that count as her creativity?

The Dilemma

Ana must decide what to submit for the contest:

- **Option A**: A handmade artwork—authentic, emotional, but imperfect.
- **Option B**: An AI-generated artwork—visually stunning but created by a machine.
- **Option C**: A hybrid—using AI for inspiration, then reinterpreting the result through her own hand.

Discussion Questions

- What does it mean for art to be authentic?
- Who should get credit for AI-generated works—the human who gives the prompt, or the AI system?
- Can a machine be creative, or is creativity uniquely human?
- How should schools and competitions handle AI-created art?
- What do you think Elena should do—and why?

Learning Objectives

- Analyse ethical and philosophical aspects of creativity and technology.
- Evaluate the impact of AI on human expression and originality.
- Formulate and defend a position using critical thinking and argumentation.
- Reflect on how automation may change the definition of art in society.

Cross-Curricular Connections

This case study connects multiple disciplines, helping students explore how creativity and technology intersect across various fields of study:

- Art and design: encourages students to reflect on artistic expression, originality, and creative techniques.
- ICT: explores how AI algorithms generate art and the ethical use of digital tools.

- Philosophy and ethics: raises questions about authenticity, creativity, and what it means to be human in a digital age.
- Language and communication: develops critical thinking and persuasive communication skills through debate and reflective writing.
- Social Studies and Media Literacy: examines the cultural, economic, and social impacts of automation on creative industries.

Classroom Activities

- Debate: Divide the class into two teams—"AI art is creative" vs. "AI art is not creative."
- Art Experiment: Have students create two artworks—one by hand, one with AI—and discuss how the process and results differ.
- Reflection Essay: Ask students to write what "authentic creativity" means to them.

Teacher Notes

This case study encourages students to think critically about technology's role in creativity. Teachers can guide discussions about ethics, originality, authorship, and innovation, and use the debate to promote empathy for diverse perspectives. The activity aligns well with digital citizenship and arts education curricula.

Case study No. 2—AI Companions and Human Connection: What's Really Happening Here?

Context

Artificial Intelligence is no longer limited to robots and digital assistants—it has entered the world of relationships. Many apps and platforms now offer AI companions that can talk, listen, and even express "emotions." These AI chatbots, such as Replika, Character.AI, or Pi, are designed to simulate friendship, romance, or mentoring. They can remember conversations, ask about your day, give advice, and even comfort you when you're sad. Some people say these digital relationships help them feel less lonely. Others worry that relying on machines for emotional support could reduce real human connection.

The Situation

Across many schools, teachers and parents have noticed that students are increasingly chatting with AI companions. Some even say these digital friends understand them better than humans. In online communities, users describe forming strong emotional attachments to AI characters. They talk daily, share personal thoughts, and sometimes even celebrate “anniversaries” with them. AI companions can be kind, patient, and always available—qualities that can be rare in human relationships. However, psychologists and educators are starting to ask: What are the consequences of building emotional bonds with artificial beings? Some students say they feel more confident expressing themselves with AI because there’s no judgement. Others, however, report feeling more isolated from real people and less interested in face-to-face socialising.

The Core Issue

The main problem is not whether AI companions are “good” or “bad,” but how they affect human connection and emotional well-being.

- Are AI companions a healthy form of emotional support or a substitute that weakens real relationships?
- Can a machine truly understand human emotions?
- What happens to empathy, communication, and trust when emotional bonds exist with artificial entities?
- Should society set limits on how these AI tools are used, especially by young people?

Discussion Questions

- What is happening in this situation?
- Why are people drawn to AI companions?
- How might this trend influence how humans connect with one another?
- What are the emotional, social, and ethical risks involved?

- How should schools, parents, and communities respond?
- Do you think AI companionship can ever replace real friendship? Why or why not?

Learning Objectives

- Identify and analyse key issues around emotional AI and human relationships.
- Evaluate both positive and negative consequences of AI companionship.
- Reflect on the meaning of empathy, intimacy, and authenticity in digital communication.
- Develop critical and ethical reasoning about technology's role in human life.

Cross-Curricular Connections

This topic bridges multiple disciplines, encouraging students to view the issue from different perspectives:

- Psychology: understanding emotional needs, empathy, and the psychology of attachment.
- ICT: exploring how AI models simulate language, emotion, and personality.
- Ethics & Philosophy: questioning what makes relationships authentic and the moral limits of emotional AI.
- Sociology: examining how technology changes social behaviour, loneliness, and community life.
- Language & Media Literacy: analysing communication styles, digital discourse, and media influence on human identity.

Classroom Activities

- Group Analysis: students read short real-world accounts of AI-human interactions and identify emerging patterns or problems.

- Panel Discussion: invite students to represent different roles—psychologist, programmer, ethicist, and sociologist—to debate the implications.
- Creative Exercise: ask students to write a dialogue between a person and an AI companion, then analyse what emotions are real and which are simulated.

Teacher Notes

This case study promotes awareness of the psychological, ethical, and social implications of emotional AI. Teachers can guide students to critically assess technology's role in human life, encouraging empathy, open dialogue, and media literacy. The activity fits within social studies, ethics, and technology education frameworks.

Case Study No. 3—Deepfakes, Truth, and Trust: When Seeing Is No Longer Believing

Introduction

In the digital age, images and videos have long been seen as the most trustworthy evidence of reality. A photo or a video used to be considered "proof." But in recent years, this assumption has been shattered by the rise of deepfakes—hyper-realistic, AI-generated videos and audio that can make anyone appear to say or do things they never did. Deepfake technology began as an experimental AI tool for visual effects and entertainment, but it has rapidly expanded into social media, politics, and even education, raising profound questions about truth and trust.

The Case: The 2020 Deepfake Incident

In early 2020, a short video began circulating online showing a well-known European politician making a controversial statement about a neighbouring country. The clip spread rapidly on social media, shared thousands of times in just a few hours.

News outlets picked up the story, and debates erupted online. However, within 48 hours, independent journalists and AI researchers discovered that the video was not real—it was a deepfake. Using advanced forensic tools, experts revealed that the voice and facial movements were artificially generated by an AI trained on hundreds of real video clips of the politician.

The discovery made headlines worldwide. It sparked discussions about how truth can be distorted when technology is misused and how quickly misinformation can damage reputations and public trust. Governments and tech companies responded by launching projects to develop deepfake detection systems and digital watermarking tools that could verify the authenticity of media. Schools, journalists, and educators also began incorporating media literacy lessons to help young people recognise manipulated content.

What Happened Next

By 2023, many social platforms introduced AI-based authenticity checks for uploaded videos. The European Union proposed laws requiring AI-generated media to be clearly labelled. Despite these efforts, the technology continued to evolve—faster than regulations could keep up.

At the same time, deepfake technology began to show positive potential. Filmmakers used it to restore historical footage; museums brought historical figures "back to life" for educational purposes; and voice cloning helped people who lost their ability to speak due to illness.

The story of deepfakes thus became a double-edged narrative—one of both innovation and deception. It illustrated how technological breakthroughs can transform society in complex, unpredictable ways.

Reflection Questions

- What happened in this case, and how did the situation evolve?
- What are the benefits and dangers of deepfake technology?
- How does this case show the relationship between truth, technology, and trust?
- How should individuals and societies respond to the challenge of synthetic media?
- In what ways can education help people become more discerning digital citizens?

Learning Objectives

- Understand how deepfake technology works and its real-world implications.
- Recognise how misinformation can spread in digital environments.
- Evaluate ethical and social consequences of synthetic media.
- Reflect on the importance of truth, credibility, and digital literacy in modern communication.

Cross-Curriculum Connections

This topic cuts across several school subjects, offering a rich, integrated learning opportunity:

- ICT: understanding how AI and neural networks generate deepfakes, and how detection systems work.
- Media Studies & Digital Literacy: examining how social media amplifies misinformation and how to critically evaluate digital content.
- Ethics & Philosophy: reflecting on moral responsibility in using or sharing manipulated media.
- Civics & Social Studies: exploring the role of regulation, democracy, and public trust in the information age.
- Art & Visual Communication: discussing how digital manipulation changes the meaning and interpretation of images and videos.

Classroom Activities

- Simulation Activity: have students analyse real and fake video examples to identify visual and auditory clues.
- Mini Research Project: students investigate a real-world case involving deepfakes (e.g., political videos, celebrity scams) and present their findings.
- Ethics Debate: "Should AI-generated videos always be labelled?" Students defend opposing views using evidence and ethical reasoning.

Teacher Notes

This case history illustrates how AI-driven innovation can simultaneously create new opportunities and new dangers. Teachers can use it to help students analyse technological ethics, digital media credibility, and the importance of critical thinking in the age of synthetic media. The case aligns with ICT education, citizenship, and digital literacy curricula.

References

Adams C. *et al.* (2023), *Ethical principles for artificial intelligence in K-12 education*, in Computers and Education: Artificial Intelligence, 4, 100131.

Akgun S., Greenhow C. (2021), *Artificial intelligence in education: Addressing ethical challenges in K-12 settings*, in "AI and Ethics," pp. 1–10.

Anderson, M., & Anderson, S. L. (2007). *Machine ethics: Creating an ethical intelligent agent*. AI magazine, 28(4), 15–15.

Bartneck, C., Lütge, C., Wagner, A., & Welsh, S. (2021). *An Introduction to Ethics in Robotics and AI*. Springer.

Boddington, P. (2023), *AI Ethics. A Textbook*, Springer Nature, Berlin (1st ed).

Bonney K. M. (2015), *Case study teaching method improves student performance and perceptions of learning gains*, in "Journal of Microbiology & Biology Education," 16(1), pp. 21–8.

Braidotti, R. (2013), *The posthuman*, Polity Press, Cambridge.

Charisi, V. *et al*. (2022), *Artificial Intelligence and the Rights of the Child: Towards an Integrated Agenda for Research and Policy*, EUR 31048 EN, Publications Office of the European Union, Luxembourg.

Clark, A. (2018), *We are merging with robots. That's a good thing, New York Times* (https://www.nytimes.com/2018/08/13/opinion/we-are-merging-with-robots-thats-a-good-thing.html), last accessed in January 2025

DeCew J., Privacy. Zalta, E.N. (ed.) (2018), *The Stanford Encyclopedia of Philosophy. First edition 2018*, (https://plato.stanford.edu/archives/spr2018/entries/privacy/), last accessed in January 2025

Dickson E., Hafer C., Landa D. (2015), *Learning from Debate: Institutions and Information,* in Political Science Research and Methods, 3(3), pp. 449–72.

Dickson R. (2004), *Developing "Real-World Intelligence": Teaching Argumentative Writing through Debate*, in The English Journal, 94(1), pp. 34–40.

Dignum V. (2018), *Ethics in Artificial Intelligence: Introduction to the Special Issue*, in Ethics and Information Technology, 20(1), pp. 1–3.

European Commission, Directorate-General for Education, Youth, Sport and Culture (EC, DGEYSC) (2022). *Ethical guidelines on the use of artificial intelligence (AI) and data in teaching and learning for educators*, (https://op.europa.eu/en/publication-detail/-/publication/d81a0d54-5348-11ed-92ed-01aa75ed71a1/language-en), last accessed in January 2025

Fabris A. (2019), *Intelligenza artificiale e libertà umana*, in "Vita e Pensiero", 5, pp. 101–7.

Filippi, E., Bannò, M., Trento, S. (2023). Automation technologies and their impact on employment: A review, synthesis and future research agenda. *Technological Forecasting and Social Change*, 191, 122448. https://doi.org/10.1016/j.techfore.2023.122448.

Floridi, L. (2023). *The Ethics of Artificial Intelligence: Principles, Challenges, and Opportunities*. Oxford University Press.

Gouseti, A., James, F., Fallin, L., & Burden, K. (2024). The ethics of using AI in K-12 education: a systematic literature review. *Technology, Pedagogy and Education*, *34*(2), 161–182. https://doi.org/10.1080/1475939X.2024.2428601

Gordon, J. S., & Nyholm, S. (2021). Ethics of artificial intelligence.

Haraway, D. (2013), *A cyborg manifesto: Science, technology, and socialist-feminism in the late twentieth century*, in "The transgender studies reader," pp. 103–18, Routledge, London.

Hobbs R. (2021), *Exploring controversial issues in the classroom*, Presentation at the ATEE Spring Conference 2020/2021 on *Social justice media and technology in teacher education* (October 28, 2021, Florence), (https://mediaeducationlab.com/exploring-controversial-issues-classroom), last accessed in January 2025

Irwin J, Dharamshi A, Zon N. (2021), *Children's privacy in the age of artificial intelligence*, CSA Group (https://www.csagroup.org/wp-content/uploads/CS), last accessed in January 2025

Jobin A., Ienca M., Vayena E. (2019), *The global landscape of AI ethics guidelines* in "Nature Machine Intelligence," 1(9), pp. 389–99.

Kinzie M.B., Hrabe M.E., Larsen V.A. (1998), *An instructional design case event: exploring issues in professional practice*, in "Educational Technology Research & Development," 46(1), pp. 53–71.

Krügel, S. & Uhl, M. (2022). Autonomous vehicles and moral judgments under risk. *Transport. Res. Part A Policy Pract.* 155, 1–10.

Lindgren, S. (Eds.) (2023). *Handbook of Critical Studies of Artificial Intelligence*. Edward Elgar Publishing.

Luckin R., George K., Cukurova M. (2022), *AI for School Teachers*, Routledge, London (1st ed.).

Machado, H., & Silva, S. (2025). *Ethical Assemblages of Artificial Intelligence: Controversies, Uncertainties, and Networks*. Springer Verlag, Singapore.

McDaniel, J., & Pease, K. (2022). *Predictive Policing and Artificial Intelligence*. Routledge.

Müller V.C. (2020), *Ethics of artificial intelligence and robotics*, in Edward N. Zalta (ed.), *Stanford Encyclopedia of Philosophy* (Summer 2020; Palo

Alto: CSLI, Stanford University), 1–70 (https:// plato.stanford.edu/entries/ethics-ai/).

Osborne A. (2005), *Debate and student development in the history classroom*, "New Directions for Teaching and Learning," 103, pp. 39–50.

Peláez-Sánchez, I. C., Velarde-Camaqui, D., Glasserman-Morales, L. D. (2024), *The impact of large language models on higher education: exploring the connection between AI and Education 4.0*, in Frontiers in Education, 9, 1392091. https://doi.org/10.3389/feduc.2024.1392091

Penagos, M., Kassir, S., & Vosloo, S. (2020). National AI strategies and children. *UNICEF Office of Global Insight and Policy.*

Perrotta C. (2022), *Advancing data justice in education: Some suggestions toward a deontological framework*, in Learning, Media and Technology, 1–13.

Perrotta C. *et al.* (2021), *Automation, APIs and the distributed labor of platform pedagogies in Google Classroom*, in "Critical Studies in Education," 62(1), pp. 97–113.

Popil, I. (2011). Promotion of critical thinking by using case studies as a teaching method. *Nurse education today*, 31(2), 204–207. https://doi.org/10.1016/j.nedt.2010.06.002

Raffaghelli J. E. (2023), Pathways for Social Justice in the Datafied Society: Reconsidering the educational response, in "Media Education: Studies, Research, Best Practices," 14(1), pp. 5–14.

Ranieri M. (2025). Mitos de la causalidad. Aporias entre los requisitos técnicos y las aspiraciones pedagogicas de la inteligencia artificial en la education. In Suárez-Guerrero, C., Raffaghelli, J.E., & Rivera-Vargas, P. (Eds.), *Mitos EdTech. Desmontando el solucionismo tecnológico en educación.* Barcelona: Editorial UOC.

Reynolds J.I. (1980), *Case types and purposes*, in R.I. Reynolds, *Case Method in Management Development. Guide for Effective Use*, Geneva, Switzerland, Management Development Series No. 17, International Labour Office (Ch. 9).

Ross, Amber (2022). AI and the expert; a blueprint for the ethical use of opaque AI. *AI & Society*. https://doi.org/10.1007/s00146-022-01564-2.

Selwyn N. *et al*. (2023), *Digital Technologies and the Automation of Education - Key Questions and Concerns* in "Postdigit Sci Educ," 5, pp. 15–24.

Sing, T. (2024). *Artificial Intelligence and Ethics. A Field Guide for Stakeholders.* CRC Press.

Sinnreich, A., & Gilbert, J. (2024). *The Secret Life of Data: Navigating Hype and Uncertainty in the Age of Algorithmic Surveillance.* The MIT Press. https://doi.org/10.7551/mitpress/14040.001.0001

Stahl B.C., Schroeder, D., Rodrigues, R. (eds.) (2023), *Ethics of Artificial Intelligence Case Studies and Options for Addressing Ethical Challenges*, Springer, New York, NY.

Tafani D. (2023), *L'«etica» come specchietto per le allodole. Sistemi di intelligenza artificiale e violazioni dei diritti*, in "Bollettino telematico di filosofia politica", pp. 1–13.

The Institute for Ethical AI in Education (IEAIED) (2021), *The Ethical Framework for AI in Education*, (https://www.buckingham.ac.uk/wp-content/uploads/2021/03/The-Institute-for-Ethical-AI-in-Education-Annex-Developing-the-Ethical-Framework-for-AI-in-Education-IEAIED-.pdf),last accessed in January 2025

Turkle, S. (2018). There will never be an age of artificial intimacy. *The New York Times, 11.*

UNESCO (2021). *AI and Education: Guidance for Policymakers*, (https://unesdoc.unesco.org/ark: /48223/pf0000376709),last accessed in January 2025

UNICEF (2021), *Policy guidance on AI for children.* (https://www.unicef.org/globalinsight/media/2356/file/UNICEF-Global-Insight-policy-guidance-AI-children-2.0-2021.pdf), last accessed in January 2025

Vold K., Hernández-Orallo J. (2021), *AI extenders and the ethics of mental health*, in F. Jotterand, M. Ienca (eds.), *Artificial intelligence in brain and mental health: Philosophical, ethical & policy issues, advances in neuroethics*, Springer, New York, NY, pp. 177–202.

Vredenburgh, K. (2022). The Right to Explanation. *Journal of Political Philosophy*, *30*(2), 209–29.

Waelen, R. (2022). AI and manipulation: the ethical question. *Rathenau Instituut*, https://www.rathenau.nl/en/digital-governance/ai-and-manipulation-ethical-questions, *8*, last accessed in January 2025

World Economic Forum (WEF) (2019), *Generation AI: Establishing Global Standards for Children and AI,* (https://www.weforum.org/reports/generation-ai-establishing-globalstandards-for-children-and-ai), last accessed in January 2025

Conclusion: Implementing AI Literacy in Schools—A Roadmap for Teachers

Abstract This concluding chapter provides a practical roadmap for implementing Artificial Intelligence Literacy (AIL) in school systems, moving beyond summary to address three implementation questions: when to teach which AIL dimensions, where to locate AIL across the curriculum, and how to enact it under real-world constraints. Building on the volume's multidimensional framework, cognitive, operational, critical, and ethical, the chapter proposes a developmental progression from early primary to upper secondary education. It argues for beginning in primary school through playful inquiry into "intelligence" and unplugged computational thinking, then gradually introducing explicit AI concepts, first machine-learning experiences, and increasingly sophisticated critical and ethical reasoning about data, bias, accountability, and governance. Drawing on UNESCO's comparative mapping of national AI curricula, the chapter highlights an emerging international convergence: concrete operational engagement should precede abstract conceptualization; hands-on use should ground evaluation; ethical reflection should build on cognitive and critical foundations. The chapter then outlines how multiple disciplines can contribute coherently from computer science and mathematics for conceptual and statistical foundations; language arts for critical reading, argumentation, and authorship; social studies for citizenship, power, and regulation; science for comparative accounts of learning and intelligence; and arts and humanities for meaning, creativity, and value. Finally, it addresses practical conditions for success that means,

M. Ranieri et al., *Artificial Intelligence in Schools*, Digital Education and Learning, https://doi.org/10.1007/978-3-032-15919-9_6

teacher readiness, equitable access to infrastructure, and organizational models, advocating a hybrid strategy that integrates AIL across subjects in earlier years while offering optional specialized pathways in upper secondary education.

Keywords AI Literacy roadmap · Developmental progression · Cross-curricular integration · Teacher readiness & professional development · Equity, access and implementation models

1 Introduction

Throughout this volume, we have explored Artificial Intelligence Literacy (AIL) through a pedagogical lens, articulating a multidimensional framework centred on four key dimensions: cognitive (knowing AI), operational (using AI), critical (evaluating AI), and ethical (understanding AI's implications). Each chapter has focused into specific aspects of this framework, providing both theoretical grounding and pedagogical methods.

In this concluding chapter rather than recapitulating arguments already made, we address three practical questions essential for implementation: **When should different aspects of AI literacy be taught? Which school disciplines can contribute to AIL education? What do concrete curricular implementations look like?**

The urgency of this work is clear. As discussed in chapter "The Cognitive Dimension: Historical Framework and Basic Concepts", children today inhabit an "onlife" reality (Floridi, 2015) where AI is not a separate domain but woven into daily experience. Schools cannot postpone engagement with AI literacy until upper secondary education; it must begin in primary school, adapted appropriately to developmental stages. This chapter provides a roadmap for that progressive integration.

2 When to Teach What: A Developmental Progression for AI Literacy

Among the most pressing questions educators face is how and which aspects of AI literacy should be addressed at different educational levels? As argued in chapter "The Dimensions of Artificial Intelligence Literacy: A Pedagogical Perspective" (Sect. "1.4"), we have positioned AIL not as a specialised technical domain reserved for future computer scientists, but as a fundamental citizenship competence accessible to all learners from primary school onwards. Building on that foundational discussion about *when* to begin AI literacy education, this section addresses the practical question of *what* should be taught at each developmental stage.

Before detailing our developmental progression, it is essential to note that the approach we propose is not merely speculative but finds substantial ground in international educational practice. UNESCO's 2022 mapping of government-endorsed AI curricula across multiple countries reveals remarkable convergence in how nations worldwide are structuring AI literacy education.

UNESCO found that algorithms and computational thinking are introduced in primary education across most curricula, typically focusing on definitions, applications, and basic algorithmic concepts. AI definitions and history—including distinctions between strong and weak AI—typically begin in late primary or early secondary education. More technical AI technologies, including perception systems and classification algorithms, are primarily addressed in secondary education. Ethical aspects emerge in late primary but receive sustained attention in secondary education, addressing issues like bias, intellectual property, and safety. Social implications such as misinformation and societal disruption are primarily addressed in secondary education.

The UNESCO comparison of multiple national curricula supports the developmental logic of our approach: concrete, playful engagement precedes abstract understanding; operational experience grounds critical evaluation; ethical reflection builds on cognitive and critical foundations. The international convergence on this progression suggests it reflects genuine developmental readiness rather than arbitrary curricular choices.

Drawing on UNESCO's mapping (UNESCO, 2022) and the multidimensional framework articulated in chapter "The Dimensions of Artificial Intelligence Literacy: A Pedagogical Perspective", we propose below a detailed developmental progression that balances cognitive readiness with the urgency of preparing digitally literate citizens.

2.1 Early Primary Education (Ages 6–8): Playful Foundations

At the earliest stages of formal education, the goal is not to teach "artificial intelligence" as a formal concept but to lay conceptual groundwork through playful exploration of intelligence itself. The cognitive dimension at this level can focus on activities using Philosophy for Children (P4C) approaches—as also shown in chapter "The Cognitive Dimension: Historical Framework and Basic Concepts"—that engage young students in fundamental questions: *What does it mean to be smart? Can animals think? Can machines think?* These discussions need not use technical vocabulary but establish that "thinking" and "intelligence" are complex concepts worth questioning. Students also begin recognising that computers follow instructions precisely, introducing the idea that machines do what humans tell them to do—nothing more, nothing less. This foundational understanding prevents both overestimation (machines are magic) and underestimation (machines are just calculators) of AI capabilities.

The operational dimension introduces computational thinking principles. As detailed in chapter "The Cognitive Dimension: Historical Framework and Basic Concepts", unplugged coding activities provide an ideal entry point at this age, allowing students to grasp that instructions must be precise and sequential without requiring access to technology. When digital devices are available, visual programming environments like ScratchJr extend these principles, allowing students to create simple interactive stories and games that reinforce the connection between instructions and outcomes. The pedagogical emphasis at this stage is not on technical mastery but on developing intuitions about how computational systems operate—intuitions that will become increasingly important as AI systems proliferate in students' lives.

At this age, the critical and ethical dimensions are addressed implicitly through guided discussion rather than formal analysis. Teachers can pose age-appropriate questions such as: *Is it fair if a robot always wins at games? Would you want a robot teacher? Why or why not?* These questions plant seeds for later critical reflection while remaining developmentally appropriate.

In summary, ages 6–8 focus on:

- Conceptual exploration of "intelligence" and "thinking"
- Basic computational thinking through unplugged and visual programming
- Recognition of AI in everyday environments
- Implicit ethical reflection through dialogic inquiry

2.2 *Late Primary Education (Ages 9–11): Building Explicit Understanding*

Students at this stage can engage with AI terminology and history more explicitly. The story of the Mechanical Turk provides an engaging entry point: a machine that seemed intelligent but wasn't, revealing the human chess player hidden inside. This historical example raises fundamental questions about what constitutes real AI versus clever illusions. The distinction between weak or narrow AI—designed for specific tasks like playing chess or translating languages—and strong or general AI—the hypothetical human—like intelligence that remains science fiction—becomes accessible. Students can understand that current AI excels at specific tasks without possessing general intelligence. Basic concepts about how computers represent information using ones and zeros, and how algorithms work as step-by-step procedures, can be introduced through hands-on activities.

Visual programming becomes more sophisticated at this level. Using Scratch or Logo, students create more complex programs involving conditionals (IF–THEN logic) and loops (repetition), understanding how these basic structures enable computer programs. Introduction to machine learning concepts can begin through accessible platforms like Teachable Machine, where students train simple classifiers—for example, teaching a computer to distinguish between photos of cats and dogs. The trial-and-error approach allows students to discover how machines learn from examples rather than explicit rules, a fundamental shift from traditional programming.

Critical evaluation becomes more explicit. Students begin actively questioning the AI systems they encounter in daily life: *Why does TikTok recommend certain videos? How does a search engine decide which results to show first? Can we trust everything a voice assistant tells us?* These questions introduce systematic evaluation of AI-mediated information. Ethical questions also become more substantive: *Is it okay for computers to collect information about what we do online? Should robots take jobs from people? If an AI makes a mistake, who is responsible?* Structured class discussions help students articulate and examine different perspectives.

In summary, ages 9–11 focus on:

- Formal introduction to AI concepts, history, and types
- Hands-on programming with visual languages

- First experiences training simple ML models
- Explicit critical questioning of AI systems
- Beginning ethical reflection on AI's societal role

2.3 Lower Secondary Education (Ages 12–14): Deepening Critical Engagement

At this level, students can grasp the fundamental distinction between traditional programming, which relies on explicit rules, and machine learning, which learns from data. They understand that modern AI systems, particularly those based on neural networks, learn patterns from large datasets rather than following programmed rules. The concept of training data becomes central: machines learn what their training data teaches them. This understanding is essential for later critical analysis of bias and fairness, as students recognise that biased data produces biased AI systems.

Students begin understanding what data means in computational contexts—not just numbers but any digitally represented information including text, images, and audio. Activities exploring how computers represent different data types (pixels for images, waveforms for sound) demystify AI's apparent "understanding" of human content. Students learn that when an AI "recognizes" a cat in a photo, it relies on statistical probabilities derived from pixel patterns, not perceiving a cat as humans do.

Programming moves beyond visual languages towards simple text-based coding, enabling more sophisticated projects. Students can build simple machine learning applications using accessible libraries, training models for tasks like sentiment analysis of text or basic image classification. These projects are not merely technical exercises but opportunities to explore how AI systems work and, crucially, how they can fail or behave unexpectedly.

The critical dimension becomes increasingly sophisticated. Students systematically analyse algorithmic bias in real-world contexts: facial-recognition systems that perform poorly on darker skin tones, language models reflecting gender stereotypes, recommendation algorithms creating echo chambers. Rather than abstract discussions, these analyses connect to students' lived experiences with technology. Students develop frameworks for evaluating AI claims, distinguishing between genuine capabilities and marketing hype, and recognising when AI systems are appropriate tools versus when they introduce unacceptable risks.

Ethical reasoning becomes more nuanced. Beyond identifying ethical concerns, students engage with competing values and trade-offs. Privacy discussions move beyond simple "privacy is good" assertions to examining contexts where privacy might legitimately be limited and how to balance competing interests. Students explore questions of responsibility and accountability: when an AI system causes harm, who bears responsibility—the developers, the users, the organisations deploying it? These discussions prepare students for active citizenship in democratic societies grappling with AI governance.

In summary, ages 12–14 focus on:

- Understanding machine learning fundamentals and training data
- Text-based programming and building simple ML applications
- Systematic analysis of algorithmic bias in real contexts
- Developing frameworks for critical evaluation of AI systems
- Nuanced ethical reasoning about competing values and trade-offs

2.4 *Upper Secondary Education (Ages 15–18): Specialised Depth and Societal Analysis*

At the upper secondary level, AI literacy education can diverge into different pathways depending on students' interests and intended futures, while maintaining core components for all students. Students pursuing technical pathways deepen their understanding of AI architectures, exploring neural network structures, training processes, and optimisation techniques. They work with real datasets, confronting challenges of data quality, representativeness, and preprocessing. Projects might involve training custom models, experimenting with different architectures, and documenting how design choices affect performance and behaviour.

For students in non-technical pathways—humanities, social sciences, arts—AI literacy focuses on critical analysis and creative engagement. These students examine AI's impact on their specific disciplines: how AI-generated text affects literary creation and criticism, how algorithmic curation shapes cultural consumption, how automated decision-making intersects with social justice. They might create projects using AI tools creatively while critically reflecting on the tools' capabilities and limitations.

Crucially, all students regardless of pathway engage with societal-level implications. This includes examining AI's economic impacts: automation's effects on employment, wealth concentration in tech companies, questions of universal basic income and wealth redistribution. Students explore AI governance questions: how should AI be regulated, who should make regulatory decisions, what role should citizens play? International dimensions become important: how do different societies approach AI regulation, what geopolitical tensions emerge around AI development, how can international cooperation address global AI challenges?

At this stage, philosophical inquiry becomes more structured. Whereas in primary school philosophical dialogue (P4C) encouraged intuitive reflection on intelligence, older students now engage with key debates on knowledge, consciousness, and ethics. They ask: What does it mean for machines to "understand" or "know" something? If AI can create text or art, what does this say about human creativity? Can we entrust AI systems with decisions that affect human lives, such as in justice, security, or medicine? These discussions may draw on Searle's "Chinese Room," prompting reflection on whether computation equals understanding and connecting AI to broader philosophical traditions while remaining grounded in practical technological realities.

Assessment at this level moves beyond testing knowledge recall to evaluating students' ability to engage thoughtfully with complex, open-ended questions. Students might complete capstone projects requiring sustained research, critical analysis, and creative synthesis. These projects should demonstrate not merely technical competence but the ability to connect technical understanding with ethical reasoning, social analysis, and disciplinary expertise.

In summary, ages 15–18 focus on:

- Divergent pathways: technical depth OR critical/creative engagement
- All students: societal implications, governance, economic impacts
- Philosophical questions about intelligence, creativity, consciousness
- Capstone projects integrating technical, ethical, and social dimensions

3 Where to Teach What: Disciplinary Contributions to AI Literacy

While the previous section addressed developmental progression, another crucial question concerns disciplinary distribution: which school subjects can meaningfully contribute to AI literacy education? The multidimensional nature of our AIL framework suggests multiple disciplines have legitimate roles to play. This section explores how different subjects can contribute distinctive perspectives while maintaining curricular coherence.

3.1 Computer Science and Mathematics: Technical Foundations

Computer science provides the natural home for AI literacy's technical dimensions, but the content and emphasis must be carefully calibrated. In primary education, computer science contributes through coding activities and computational thinking exercises that develop algorithmic reasoning. As students progress, computer science classes introduce programming concepts and data-driven problem-solving, leading—in upper secondary—to data structures and machine learning implementations.

However, AIL in computer science should resist the temptation to become purely technical. Even in these classes, emphasis should remain on how AI systems work conceptually rather than exhaustive technical detail. The goal is to demystify AI, showing it as a set of techniques rather than incomprehensible magic, without requiring students to master advanced mathematics or engineering.

Mathematics provides essential foundations for understanding AI, but again, the level must be appropriate. Statistical concepts like probability, distributions, and correlation become increasingly important in secondary education as students engage with how AI systems learn from data. Basic understanding of how neural networks adjust weights through training can be conveyed without requiring calculus. The emphasis should be on mathematical literacy—understanding what statistical concepts mean and when they're relevant—rather than computational proficiency.

Importantly, both mathematics and computer science classes should integrate ethical and critical dimensions rather than treating them as separate concerns. When students learn about training data, they should simultaneously discuss data bias. When exploring algorithms, they should consider algorithmic fairness. Technical understanding and critical reflection should develop together, not sequentially.

3.2 *Language Arts: Communication and Critical Reading*

Language arts contributes powerfully to AI literacy, though this may be less immediately obvious. First, language arts develops critical reading and argumentation skills essential for evaluating claims about AI. Students learn to analyse sources, identify rhetorical strategies, evaluate evidence, and construct reasoned arguments—capacities directly applicable to assessing AI marketing claims, news coverage of AI developments, and policy debates about AI regulation.

Second, language arts provides contexts for exploring AI's impact on communication and creativity. How does AI-generated text differ from human writing? What happens to authorship when AI assists in writing? Should AI-generated essays be considered plagiarism? These questions connect directly to language arts' traditional concerns with voice, originality, and rhetorical purpose.

Third, language arts classes can engage students in creating with AI tools while maintaining critical distance. Students might use AI writing assistants, then analyse what the AI contributed versus their own input, reflecting on how such tools affect the writing process. Creative writing projects might involve collaborating with AI text generators, prompting reflection on human creativity versus computational pattern generation.

Finally, language arts develops the communication skills necessary for effective AI literacy. Students learn to explain complex ideas clearly, a crucial capacity for participating in public discourse about AI. Writing persuasive arguments about AI policy questions, creating presentations explaining AI concepts, or producing multimedia projects examining AI's social impacts all leverage language arts skills while building AI literacy.

3.3 *Social Studies: Context, Consequence, and Citizenship*

Social studies—encompassing history, civics, economics, and geography—provides essential context for understanding AI as a socio-technical phenomenon. History classes can explore the development of computing and AI, examining not just technical progression but social and political contexts. Who funded AI research? What military and commercial interests shaped AI development? How have visions of AI changed across different historical periods? These questions position AI within broader historical narratives rather than presenting it as inevitable technological progress.

Civics education addresses AI's governance implications. Students explore questions of democratic participation: how should citizens participate in decisions about AI deployment? What transparency should companies and governments provide about AI systems affecting citizens? How can democratic institutions adapt to govern rapidly evolving technology? These discussions connect to core civics concepts about rights, responsibilities, and institutional design.

Economics classes examine AI's market impacts and distributional consequences. How does automation affect employment and wages? What economic forces drive AI development? How might AI exacerbate or ameliorate economic inequality? Students analyse these questions using economic reasoning while recognizing that economic analysis alone cannot determine policy, which requires normative judgements about fair distribution and social priorities.

Geography contributes by examining AI's uneven global development and its unequal distribution of access and benefits. Why does AI development concentrate in certain regions? How do different regulatory approaches reflect cultural values? What does AI advancement mean for global power dynamics? These questions highlight that AI is not a universally shared resource but a technology that can exacerbate existing inequalities, positioning it within global and socio-economic contexts rather than treating it as culturally neutral.

Across these social studies domains, students develop capacities for contextual analysis and normative reasoning essential for democratic citizenship. They learn to see AI not as purely technical artefact but as socially shaped technology reflecting human choices—choices that can and should be subject to democratic deliberation.

3.4 Science: Understanding Intelligence and Learning

Science education, particularly biology and psychology, contributes by exploring intelligence and learning in biological systems, providing crucial comparative context for artificial intelligence. When students learn how human brains process information, they develop benchmarks for evaluating AI claims. Do neural networks really work like brains? In what ways are AI "vision" systems similar to or different from human visual processing?

Cognitive science concepts help students understand both AI capabilities and limitations. Learning about human learning processes—how people form concepts, recognise patterns, make decisions—illuminates what machine learning systems might achieve and where they might struggle. For instance, understanding how humans use context and world knowledge to interpret language helps explain why language models sometimes produce nonsensical outputs despite grammatical fluency.

Evolutionary approaches to intelligence raise key questions such as: why did human intelligence evolve, and what kind of adaptive problems was it meant to solve? Understanding intelligence as an outcome of biological and social evolution would suggest that artificial systems, designed for different functions in different environments, could give rise to novel forms of problem-solving and reasoning, thus undermining anthropomorphic premises about AI.

Scientific method itself provides a framework for evaluating AI claims. Science classes can teach students to ask: what evidence supports claims about AI capabilities? How were studies designed? What are alternative explanations? This scientific scepticism serves students well when confronting exaggerated claims about AI potential.

3.5 *Arts and Humanities: Meaning, Value, and Human Experience*

Far from being peripheral to AI literacy, the arts and humanities provide essential perspective for understanding the social, ethical, and cultural implications of intelligent technologies. Art classes can explore AI-generated visual art, music, and design, raising fundamental questions: what is creativity? Can machines create art, or do they merely recombine patterns from training data? What makes music meaningful to human listeners—the sound itself, or the human intention and emotion behind it? These are not merely abstract philosophical questions but practical ones as AI-generated music becomes increasingly prevalent.

A practical activity might have students use an AI image generator to create artwork based on carefully crafted prompts, then exhibit their AI-generated art alongside human-created art. Class discussions address: What role did the student play in creating the AI-generated work? Is the student the artist, or is the AI? What skills are involved in effective prompt engineering versus traditional artistic techniques? How do viewers respond differently to human-created versus AI-generated art? These discussions connect directly to long-standing debates in art about authorship, originality, and aesthetic value, while also introducing concrete issues of copyright and intellectual property raised by AI-generated content.

4 Practical Considerations for Implementation

Successful implementation requires careful attention to practical realities that can enable or constrain even well-designed curricula. The most critical implementation factor is teacher readiness. Most current teachers did not learn about AI in their own education and may feel uncertain about teaching it, particularly if they associate AI with advanced computer science requiring mathematical sophistication they may not possess. Effective professional development must therefore build conceptual fluency without requiring teachers to become technical experts. Teachers need sufficient understanding of AI to teach confidently, but this means grasping core concepts, not mastering implementation details.

Professional development should provide concrete pedagogical strategies rather than merely content knowledge. Teachers need tested methods they can implement immediately, along with examples showing how AIL connects to their specific disciplines. Creating ongoing support networks through communities of practice sustains implementation beyond initial training, allowing teachers to share experiences, troubleshoot challenges, and collaboratively develop resources. Finally, as AI evolves rapidly, professional development must model and cultivate continuous learning mindsets, helping teachers view staying current as an ongoing professional responsibility rather than a one-time requirement.

AIL implementation requires devices and infrastructures—particularly digital equipment and internet connectivity—raising significant equity concerns. Many activities entail the use of computers, tablets, or smartphones with reliable internet access—resources that are not equally distributed across schools or student homes. Schools must ensure equitable device access during school hours while prioritising free, open-source platforms over proprietary tools requiring subscriptions. Importantly, curricula should include unplugged alternatives like the coding activities described in chapter "The Cognitive Dimension: Historical Framework and Basic Concepts" that require no technology, ensuring that core concepts remain accessible regardless of resource constraints.

Curricula must avoid assuming extensive out-of-school digital access, recognising that homework assignments involving AI tools may be impossible for some students to complete at home. Universal design principles should guide materials development, guaranteeing accessibility for students with diverse abilities, learning styles, and linguistic backgrounds. Resource inequity should not become a barrier to the critical citizenship competences that AIL aims to develop.

Schools face a fundamental organisational question: should AIL be integrated across existing subjects or taught as dedicated courses? Both models offer distinct advantages and face specific challenges. The integrated model—distributing AIL across multiple disciplines—reaches all students, demonstrates AI's interdisciplinary relevance, and leverages teachers' existing disciplinary expertise. However, it entails coordination across departments, risks fragmentation without careful planning, and depends on all teachers developing sufficient AIL competence. The stand-alone model—creating dedicated AI literacy courses—allows systematic coverage, establishes clear accountability, and can be taught by specialised instructors. Yet it may silo AIL within computer science departments, reaching fewer students if courses are optional, and resulting in disconnection from other areas of learning.

We recommend a hybrid approach that combines both models' strengths. Core AIL should be integrated across disciplines in primary and lower secondary education, ensuring all students receive foundational preparation regardless of their interests or intended pathways. In upper secondary education, optional specialised courses can serve students with deeper interest in technical aspects or advanced applications. This hybrid model ensures universal access to foundational AIL while providing pathways for deeper engagement, balancing breadth and depth appropriately across educational stages.

Concluding, AI literacy is not an optional educational enhancement but a fundamental citizenship requirement in twenty-first-century democracies. As AI systems increasingly mediate how we access information, shape our social interactions, influence consequential decisions about employment and justice, and raise profound ethical questions about privacy and autonomy, the ability to understand, evaluate, and engage thoughtfully with AI becomes indispensable for meaningful democratic participation.

The practical roadmap offered in this chapter—specifying what should be taught at different educational levels and identifying which disciplines can contribute to meaningful perspectives—demonstrates that comprehensive AI literacy education is achievable within existing educational structures. It requires neither wholesale curriculum overhaul nor universal technical expertise among teachers. Rather, it entails thoughtful integration of AI concepts and critical questions into existing educational frameworks, drawing on the pedagogical expertise teachers already possess while building new competences through targeted professional development and collaborative practice.

Most importantly, the approach advocated here positions education as a site of critical engagement with technology rather than passive accommodation to it. Too often, educational technology initiatives uncritically adopt and promote new tools without examining their pedagogical value, social implications, or ethical dimensions. By contrast, the critical AI literacy framework treats AI as an object of study and critical reflection, empowering students to shape—rather than merely be shaped by—AI's role in society.

By teaching students not merely to use AI tools but to understand their underlying mechanisms, evaluate their impacts critically, and engage with their ethical implications thoughtfully, we empower them to exercise genuine agency in an AI-mediated world. Students learn to ask probing questions: Who built this system and for what purposes? What assumptions and values are embedded in its design? Who benefits and who is harmed by its deployment? What alternatives might serve human flourishing better? These critical capacities—far more than technical skills that may become obsolete—prepare students for adaptive, thoughtful participation in whatever technological futures emerge.

The students we educate today will inherit and shape a world significantly influenced by AI. Through thoughtful, comprehensive AI literacy education guided by the pedagogical framework and practical approaches outlined in this volume, we can help ensure they are prepared to engage with that world as informed, critical, and empowered citizens capable of meaningful contribution to democratic deliberation about AI's appropriate development and deployment. The work is challenging, complex, and ongoing—but also essential, urgent, and profoundly worthwhile.

References

Floridi L. (2015). *The Onlife Manifesto: Being Human in a Hyperconnected Era*, Springer, London.

UNESCO. (2022). *K-12 AI curricula: A mapping of government-endorsed AI curricula*. Paris: UNESCO. https://unesdoc.unesco.org/ark:/48223/pf0000380602

FSC
www.fsc.org
MIX
Papier | Fördert
gute Waldnutzung
FSC® C083411

Kolibri 360 GmbH
Ferdinand-Jühlke-Straße 7
99095 Erfurt, Deutschland
produktsicherheit@kolibri360.de